Night Journey
and
Ascension

Javed Ahmed Ghamidi's Stance

On Prophet Muhammad's

Night Journey

and

Ascension

Derived from a dialogue with Muhammad Hassan Ilyas

Compiled by

SYED MANZOOR-UL-HASSAN

Ghamidi Center
of Islamic Learning
An Initiative of Al-Mawrid US Inc.

**Ghamidi Center
of Islamic Learning**
An Initiative of Al-Mawrid US Inc.

First Edition: May 2025
ISBN: 978-1-966600-25-1
Publisher: Ghamidi Center of Islamic Learning, Al-Mawrid US
Address: 3620 N Josey Ln, Suite 230, Carrollton, TX 75007 USA
Website: www.ghamidicenter.com
Email: info@almawridus.org

Table of Contents

Our Approach to Translate Academic Works for A Global Audience

The translation of this book from Urdu to English is conducted by Al-Mawrid US Translations team, employing a state-of-the-art Artificial Intelligence (AI) to ensure initial accuracy and fluency in translation. Following the AI translation phase, each book undergoes a meticulous review process executed by our specialized review team. This team, composed of proficient speakers of both the original and translated languages, conducts a comprehensive proofreading, editing and validation of each sentence to ensure the translation meets the highest standards of accuracy and cultural sensitivity.

Our rigorous review process is designed to preserve the original text's nuances, ensuring that readers experience the author's intent, style, and voice in English as authentically as possible. The reviewers pay close attention to idiomatic expressions, cultural references, and the subtleties of language that AI might not fully capture, adjusting as necessary to convey the true essence and nature of the original work.

We take pride in our thorough approach, which combines the effect of modern technology with the discerning expertise of human reviewers. By including this section in our books, we aim to inform our readers about the meticulous care and effort invested in bringing these translations to life, ensuring transparency and fostering trust in the quality of our work.

Contributors and Book-Specific Notes

For this particular volume, the translation project was managed under the supervision of Mukaram Aziz, who was responsible for the technical automation of the AI-driven translation process, overall layout design and textual presentation, and the final editorial review. Abid Mehmood conducted the initial review and was responsible for validating the accuracy of Arabic language content throughout the book. Azeem Ayub oversaw the final formatting to ensure consistency and readability in the published edition. The cover design is created by Crayonz Media

The original Arabic text is included only for Qur'anic and hadith references. The English translation of Qur'anic verses is derived from Dr. Shehzad Saleem's translation of Al-Bayān. The hadith texts were translated from Urdu as they appeared in the original manuscript of this book.

To make the text more accessible to English-speaking readers, terms and phrases in other languages—particularly Arabic, Urdu and Persian—have been transliterated when they appear in the text. We followed the IJMES transliteration style as a reference but adopted a simplified subset of characters (primarily ā, ī, ') to reflect Arabic pronunciation while maintaining readability. In keeping with convention and out of reverence, the following abbreviations are used: PBUH (Peace be upon him) for all prophets, RA (Radi Allāhu anhu/anhā) for the Companions of the Prophet, and AS (alayhi/alayhā al-salām) for other noble personalities.

This work, while rigorous, remains a human endeavor and may still contain occasional errors or oversights. We welcome feedback and suggestions for improvement at translations@almawridus.org.

In the name of God,
the Most Gracious, the Ever Merciful

Preface

*I*sra and *Mi'raj* translates to 'The Night Journey and Ascension.' *Isra* refers to the Prophet Muhammad's (PBUH) night journey from Mecca to Jerusalem, and *Mi'raj* refers to his ascension to the heavens, both of which are significant concepts in Islamic tradition.

This book presents the stance of my revered teacher, Javed Ahmed Ghamidi. It has been extracted from episodes 34 to 37 of the video series 'Response to 23 Questions on Religious Opinions of Javed Ahmed Ghamidi.' This series of discussions addresses the objections commonly raised against Javed Ahmed Ghamidi's thoughts from the perspective of traditional approaches to the study and interpretation of Islam and presents his unique stances in contrast to the consensus views of traditional scholarship. These views, often presented as the consensus views of the *ummah*, are actually prevalent interpretations of various debates around individual matters about the Qur'an, the Sunnah, Hadith and *Seerah* (biographical accounts of the Prophet). Javed Ahmed Ghamidi has partially or entirely dismissed these purportedly unanimous views. He found them to be in conflict with the facts found within the Qur'an's texts and the practices known as the Sunnah, as well as with the acknowledged facts in the fields of Hadith and *Seerah*.

The discussions follow the method of question-and-answer and interactive dialogue. Muhammad Hassan Ilyas participates in the conversation as Javed Ahmed Ghamidi's interlocutor. He has comprehensively organized all the issues that have been presented as controversial views of Javed Ahmed Ghamidi and has faithfully and eloquently presented them before the teacher. In response, the teacher has elucidated the traditional viewpoints further, analyzed the arguments of traditional scholars, and presented his own stance, thoroughly substantiated with full clarity.

I have taken up the responsibility to compile and present the series of discussions in the form of monographs. To meet the needs of professional writing, I have divided the detailed and long discussions into sections, explained the allusions, and explicated the terse statements which might sound ambiguous to some readers. Where appropriate, relevant excerpts from Javed Ahmed Ghamidi's writings have been quoted. These writings enrich the discussion through further explication of, elaboration upon, support to, and emphasis upon significant points borrowed from the works of erudite scholars of great repute and stature. The purpose of this exercise is to present the audio-visual records of the highly useful and instructive discussions in writing so that students and researchers have ready access to this source and benefit from it. Shahid Mahmood has provided support in compilation and research, executing this responsibility with utmost diligence.

These articles are essentially my understanding of Javed Ahmed Ghamidi's thoughts and views. However, fortunately, Javed Ahmed Ghamidi has been kind enough to read and revise them. As a result, my prominent mistakes in understanding his views are corrected on the one hand and the style of presentation is reformed on the other.

It is an honor for me to infer the scholarly discussions on religious themes from my mentor's verbal discussions and it is definitely a great privilege to have his principal guidance in this onerous task. This is a boundless favor from God Almighty, which definitely surpasses the measures of my ability and capability. All praise is due to Allah.

The aforementioned video series and articles based on those discussions are being organized and arranged by Ghamidi Center of Islamic Learning, Al-Mawrid US. May Allah accept this collective effort by the organization and the individuals involved. Amen.

Introduction

The incident of *Isra and Mi'raj*[1] is seen as an extraordinary miracle of Prophet Muhammad, peace be upon him. Exegetes, traditionalists, and biographers base their descriptions of this event on Verses 1 and 60 of Surah Al-Isra, Verses 1 to 18 of Surah Al-Najm, and numerous traditions from the Hadith literature. Surah Al-Isra recounts that the Prophet (PBUH) was transported overnight from the Masjid al-Haram to the Masjid Al-Aqsa, to witness some of Allah's signs. Surah Al-Najm relates that the Prophet saw the Angel Gabriel in his true form twice, once near the higher horizon and another time by *Sidrat al-Muntaha* (The Lote Tree at the Farthest Limit). At the higher horizon, there was also an encounter where the proximity was described as *Qāba Qawsayn* (two bow lengths).

The hadiths recount that one night, Gabriel the Trusted, came to the Prophet (PBUH), split his chest open, filled it with wisdom and faith, and then closed it. Afterward, the lightning-speed steed, Buraq, was brought forth. The Prophet (PBUH) mounted Buraq and journeyed towards Jerusalem. Upon journeying over various terrestrial landmarks and arriving in Jerusalem, he tied the Buraq outside the mosque and entered the temple constructed by Solomon where all the prophets had already gathered for prayer. The Prophet (PBUH) led the prayer, and all prophets prayed in congregation behind him. For hospitality, two bowls, one carrying milk and the other filled with wine were offered to him; he opted for the milk and drank it. Following this, a ladder was erected for his ascension to the heavens, which he then ascended. Gabriel was with him throughout this journey. Sequentially, he traversed the seven heavens, encountering prophets at each level - including Adam, Abraham, Idris, Joseph,

---

[1] The word *Isra* has been derived from the words *asra bi abdihī* (He took his servant) from Surah Al-Isra. The word *Mi'raj* has been adopted from the words *urija bi* (I was taken to the heavens) appearing in a hadith narrative. *Mi'raj* is the arabic word for ladder.

Moses, Aaron, John, and Jesus, peace be upon them all. Beyond the seventh heaven, he ascended higher and arrived at the very boundary separating human and divine realms - *Sidrat al-Muntaha*. There, Gabriel's journey came to a halt, and the Prophet (PBUH) continued alone. At last, he was in the direct presence of the Divine Court. In this place, he was graced with ultimate closeness to Allah (*Qāba Qawsayn*). Allah then bestowed upon him the commandment for fifty daily prayers. With this decree, he commenced his return journey. Moses (PBUH), whom he met on the seventh heaven, recommended a reduction in the number of prayers, drawing on his experience with his nation. Heeding this advice, the Prophet (PBUH) returned to the Divine Court and requested a reduction in the allocated number of prayers, which was granted. As he descended again, Moses (PBUH) repeated the advice.

The Prophet (PBUH) returned to the Divine Court again. Moses (PBUH) continued to advise further reductions until the commandment was abated to five daily prayers. Upon Moses's (PBUH) suggestion for further reductions, the Prophet (PBUH) deemed it inappropriate to seek more leniency. Thus, with this divine gift, the Prophet (PBUH) then headed for the world and traversed down through the heavens, re-entered Jerusalem, led the prophets in prayer once again, mounted Buraq, and returned to the Sacred Mosque (Masjid al-Haram).

During this miraculous journey, the Prophet (PBUH) was shown the heavenly pond of *Kawthar*, the Frequented House (*Bayt al-Ma'mur*), and glimpses of both paradise and hell. Some scholars maintain that at the closeness of 'two bow lengths,' he was also blessed with the esteemed vision of beholding Allah Almighty. All these occurrences unfolded while he was fully awake, and the Prophet Muhammad, (PBUH), experienced and witnessed these events in both spiritual and physical forms[2].

---

[2] In general, most scholars agree on the occurrence of these events of *Mi'raj*. However, some of these details are based on certain hadith narratives that

This text summarizes the information that is widely accepted and acknowledged as part of the events known as *Isra* and *Mi'raj* in our scholarly tradition. The details are derived from interpretations of the Qur'an, explanations of hadith, biographical accounts of the Prophet (*seerah*), and specific works on *Dalail al-Nubuwwah* (Proofs of Prophethood) and *Mu'jizat al-Nabi* (Miracles of the Prophet).

Javed Ahmed Ghamidi regards the events of *Isra* and *Mi'raj* as *ayātun min ayāti Allah* (a few among the signs of Allah) and acknowledges their miraculous and supernatural nature. Yet, he disagrees with the conventional interpretation. He contends that traditional explanations lack proper understanding, reasoning, and exposition. These interpretations, he argues, often misrepresent the actual meanings intended by the Qur'an and hadith. Consequently, he has undertaken a critical evaluation of this traditional view, scrutinized its premises, and presented a dissenting opinion.

The book details his critique and stance through two main chapters and several appendices. The first chapter is titled 'Javed Ahmed Ghamidi's Position' and affirms the scholar's perspective by interpreting Qur'anic texts and hadith, outlining the events in context, forming coherent arguments, and listing the findings in a structured manner. The second chapter critiques the conventional belief and is called 'Traditional Position and Its Critical Review'. It starts by positively citing the traditional accounts and their logical consequences, bringing forward the claims of its adherents. Subsequently, in a summarized manner, it elucidates the foundations upon which Javed Ahmed Ghamidi's critical analysis is based. Then, it methodically addresses and identifies the shortcomings in the traditional arguments and conclusions under various headings:

- Single Incident or Four Separate Incidents?
- The Meaning of Al-Ru'ya in Relation to Isra — Traditional Position

---

have been declared weak by the hadith experts. The scholars accept their weakness but consider them in line with the Qur'an and the sound hadiths; to conclude that they must be accepted.

- Conclusive Evidence in the Debate over Physical or Spiritual Journey
- The Meaning and Concept of al-Ru'ya
- Reality of Citing Al-Mutanabbi's Verse as Evidence
- Reality of Citing Al- Ra'i's Verse as Evidence
- Intended Meaning of the Phrase *Subḥān alladhī*
- Reality of the Argument Based on *Asra bi 'abdihi*
- Argument Based on the Report from Abdullah Ibn Abbas
- Argument Based on the Phrase *Fitnatan lilnās*
- Argument Based on People's Reactions
- The Concept of Seeing Allah Almighty

The book concludes with appendices containing vital supplementary discussions and explanations for readers seeking deeper understanding or reference to the sources of the debates.

Chapter One

Javed Ahmed Ghamidi's Position

Traditionally, the *Isra* and *Mi'raj* are believed to be the same event. The diverse details narrated in the Qur'an and hadith are considered parts of the single event. As a result, it is generally believed that the Prophet's night journey was one particular event that occurred at night, in a state of wakefulness, began from Masjid al-Haram, proceeded to Masjid Al-Aqsa, and culminated at the highest assembly.

Javed Ahmed Ghamidi, however, disagrees with this traditional viewpoint, arguing that the texts of the Qur'an and hadith do not support it. He believes that these were not one but four distinct events that occurred on different occasions, took different forms, and happened in different states of consciousness. The textual evidence from the Qur'an and hadith clearly proves that they are separate independent events. Additionally, he suggests that not all these events took place in the state of Prophet Muhammad's (PBUH) wakefulness. Two of them happened in the realm of dreams (*al-ru'ya*), and two occurred in an awakened state.

- The first event is the *Isra*, which is described in Surah Al-Isra of the Holy Qur'an, and occurred in a dream.

- The second event is the encounter at the *Sidrat al-Muntaha* (The Lote Tree at the Farthest Limit), mentioned in verses 1 to 12 of Surah Al-Najm, and took place in a state of wakefulness.

- The third event is described in verses 13 to 18 of Surah Al-Najm and relates to *Qāba Qawsayn*, also happening in an awakened state.

1

- Lastly, the fourth[3] event of *Mi'raj* is recorded in Sahih Bukhari, No. 7517, and other narrations, concluding that it transpired within a dream.

These four incidents are from Allah. Their nature is that of divine signs, and their significance is of revelation and inspiration. The mentioned reports, information, events, and observations are related to the prophethood and messengership of the Prophet (PBUH). Thus, they should be understood in this context and interpreted accordingly. In this matter, it is essential to stay confined to the understanding of the texts. Therefore, one should not speculate about these events, make them subject to storytelling, or search for ways to deny them by basing arguments on raw and incomplete human knowledge and experiences.

~~~~~~~~~~

1. The Incident of *Isra* (Journey to Masjid Al-Aqsa)

سُبْحٰنَ الَّذِىٓ اَسْرٰى بِعَبْدِهٖ لَيْلًا مِّنَ الْمَسْجِدِ الْحَرَامِ اِلَى الْمَسْجِدِ الْاَقْصَا الَّذِىٓ بَارَكْنَا حَوْلَهٗ لِنُرِيَهٗ مِنْ اٰيٰتِنَاؕ اِنَّهٗ هُوَ السَّمِيْعُ الْبَصِيْرُؕ

Flawless is the being who one night took His servant from the Sacred Mosque to that Distant Mosque whose surroundings We have blessed so that We can make him observe some of Our signs. Indeed, only He hears and knows all. (17:1)

وَمَا مَنَعَنَآ اَنْ نُّرْسِلَ بِالْاٰيٰتِ اِلَّآ اَنْ كَذَّبَ بِهَا الْاَوَّلُوْنَؕ وَاٰتَيْنَا ثَمُوْدَ النَّاقَةَ مُبْصِرَةً فَظَلَمُوْا بِهَاؕ وَمَا نُرْسِلُ بِالْاٰيٰتِ اِلَّا تَخْوِيْفًا. وَاِذْ قُلْنَا لَكَ اِنَّ رَبَّكَ اَحَاطَ بِالنَّاسِؕ وَمَا جَعَلْنَا الرُّءْيَا الَّتِىٓ اَرَيْنٰكَ اِلَّا فِتْنَةً لِّلنَّاسِ وَالشَّجَرَةَ الْمَلْعُوْنَةَ فِى الْقُرْاٰنِؕ وَنُخَوِّفُهُمْۙ فَمَا يَزِيْدُهُمْ اِلَّا طُغْيَانًا كَبِيْرًا.

What has stopped Us from sending signs of punishment is that the earlier generations had denied them. We had given the

---

[3] This is a descriptive sequence, not a chronological one.

Thamūd a she-camel [in a similar way] as an eye-opening sign but they were unjust to themselves and denied it. [What then is the use to send signs?] We only send signs to frighten [people before punishing them]. Remember when [for such an admonition and warning,] We said to you: Your Lord has surrounded these people; [and they were making fun of this]. The dream We showed you We made it a trial too for these people [because of this attitude of theirs] and that tree as well which has been cursed in the Qur'an. We are only frightening them of their fate, but this thing is merely increasing them in their extreme rebelliousness. (17:59-60)

Background

In verse 1 of Surah Al-Isra, 'Sacred Mosque' refers to the Kaaba in Mecca and 'Farthest Mosque' refers to the Al-Aqsa Mosque in Jerusalem. Both mosques were constructed by Allah's command and designated as the centers for the call to monotheism. Consequently, they have always remained under the custody of the descendants of Prophet Abraham (PBUH), including the surrounding areas of Mecca and Palestine. Custodianship and trust of the Kaaba and Mecca, the mother of towns, was conferred upon the Ishmaelites, and the administration of the Al-Aqsa Mosque and the authority over the land of Palestine was given to the Israelites. When Prophet Muhammad (PBUH), was sent as a messenger among the Ishmaelites, and the Israelites were relieved from the duty of calling to religion and bearing witness,[4] Allah decided to entrust both Mecca and the land of

---

[4] In Surah Aale Imran, verse 26, Allah Almighty instructed the Prophet (PBUH) to pray in this context. The verse states:

[Their era has ended; so, now] pray you: "God! The Sovereign of all sovereignty, You grant sovereignty to whomsoever You please and take it away from whomsoever You please. And You grant honour to whomsoever You please and humiliate whomsoever You please. All good lies in Your control alone; Indeed, You have power over all things.

Under this verse, Javed Ahmed Ghamidi writes in the commentary:

Palestine to Prophet Muhammad (PBUH) and his nation, the Ishmaelites. This is the historical background in which the Prophet (PBUH) was taken to the Al-Aqsa Mosque.

Details

The Qur'an narrates the incident of the *Isra* briefly, without mentioning specific details except for the nature and purpose. The stated points are as follows:

Firstly, that one night, Allah took His Prophet from the Sacred Mosque to the Al-Aqsa Mosque—a mosque far distant[5], hundreds of miles away.

Secondly, Allah's purpose in taking him there was to show him some of His extraordinary signs. This meaning is implied in the words *li nuriya hu min ayatina* (to show him some of Our signs) without detailing these signs[6]. However, based on the contextual indicators and other parallels in the Qur'an, it is plausible that these include the divine signs, evidence, heavenly lights, and blessings that filled these two abodes. Presumably, the intent of showing these to the Prophet was to give him the good news that the guardianship of these centers

---

This appears to be a prayer, but upon reflection, it contains a profound glad tiding for the Ishmaelites. This is because the prayer clearly indicates that the Lord of all good, the Sustainer of the worlds, has decided to grant sovereignty of the world to the Ishmaelites, and no opposition from the Israelites can overturn this decision. For them, there is nothing but disgrace. Thus, if they are to remain in this world, it will only be under the subjugation of the Ishmaelites. There is no other way of survival left for them. (Al-Bayan 1/335).

[5] It was located approximately 1,300 kilometers from the Sacred Mosque in Makkah, about a 40-day journey. It is introduced with the words 'al-Masjid Al-Aqsa'—meaning 'the farthest mosque'—to easily direct the audience's attention toward it.

[6] The reason is that neither can those signs be comprehended by human knowledge and intellect, nor can words bear the burden of describing their details.

of monotheism was about to be entrusted to him. Imam Amin Ahsan Islahi comments:

> *The apparent purpose of displaying these (signs) is to make it clear that it is the will of Allah Almighty that from then on, this trust would be taken away from the ungrateful and the betrayers and entrusted to him (Prophet Muhammad (PBUH)). (Tadabbur-e-Qur'an 4/475)*

The third point is that the event of the Prophet's (PBUH) journey from Masjid al-Haram to Masjid Al-Aqsa and the presentation of the signs of Allah to him occurred in a dream. The words from Surah Al-Isra, verse 60, *Wa mā ja'alnā al-ru'yā allatī araynāka* (The dream We showed you...) support this.

The summary can be outlined in a few key points as follows:

1. This event occurred at night.

2. At that time, the Prophet (PBUH) was in Masjid al-Haram.

3. Allah Almighty transported him from Masjid al-Haram to a distant mosque, namely, Al-Aqsa Mosque.

4. The purpose was to exhibit some of the signs of Allah to him.

5. This journey, which would normally require about 80 days of travel, and the witnessing of Allah's signs, were both completed within a single night.

6. This journey took place in the realm of a dream, meaning that the Prophet (PBUH) was asleep in Masjid al-Haram, and Allah Almighty made him experience this journey in this state[7].

7. The dream signifies that the entire journey and the accompanying observations were not physical but were manifested spiritually and emotionally.

---

[7] A detailed discussion on the topic of *Rū'ya* (dream) is presented in the following pages under the heading 'The Meaning of Al-Ru'ya in Relation to Isra — Traditional Position.'

The points that are not mentioned in the event are as follows:

1. It is not mentioned whether Allah Almighty Himself guided the Prophet (PBUH) to the journey or if He assigned the task to His angel.

2. There is no mention of whether the Prophet (PBUH) traveled on any physical means of transportation or if his spiritual existence carried out Allah's command.

3. No details about the signs shown to the Prophet (PBUH) have been mentioned.

4. No mention of the events happening inside Al-Aqsa Mosque has been made.

Explanation

The important points for the explanation and understanding of the verses are:

Firstly, verse 1 commences with the words *Subhāna alladhī* and ends with *innahu huwa samīʿu al-basīr*. The terms translate to 'Exalted is He' and 'Allah is the All-Hearing, the All-Seeing.' These attributes of 'hearing and seeing' essentially expound the term *Subhān*. They explicate the ultimate purpose of the event of *Isra* with great precision. Javed Ahmed Ghamidi states in Al-Bayan:

> *These attributes explain the way the word Subhān occurs at the beginning of the verse. The implication is that since God hears and knows all, hence it is His responsibility to bring to account the people who had gone back on their promises and who in the words of Jesus (PBUH) had made his House 'a den of robbers,' (Matthew, 21:13). This had to happen after hearing and reading what the Israelites said and did in it. Thus the Almighty decided that this House was to be entrusted to the custody of His last prophet. It was because of this reason that he was brought here from the Sacred Mosque in one night. God is free of all defects; hence He cannot in the slightest tolerate that He choose a nation to conclusively communicate the truth to people and leave it*

unaccountable in spite of such rebelliousness from it. It was essential that He make some other arrangement to realize this objective. He thus chose the Ishmaelites to carry out the obligation of preaching and conclusively communicating the truth at the global level. (Al-Bayan 3/63)

Secondly, the phrase *alladhī bāraknā hawlahu* (Whose precincts We have blessed) from the same verse implies that it is not merely the charge of Masjid Al-Aqsa being referred to, but also the governance over the region wherein this mosque stands. Similarly, the words *linuriyahu min ayātinā* (to show him of Our signs) suggest that among the signs, authority over the land of Palestine is also encompassed. Javed Ahmed Ghamidi writes:

After the migration of Prophet Abraham (PBUH) from Babylon, Allah Almighty selected two places, at which, by His command, two mosques were established, and they were designated as centers for the propagation of monotheism for the entire world. One is located in the land of Arabia and the other in Palestine. The first spot is a valley that is barren, and the second is exceedingly fertile. For this reason, it has been called the 'Land of Milk and Honey' in ancient scriptures. The Qur'an alludes to this with the expression 'alladhī bāraknā hawlahu', specifically denoting that the remote mosque being mentioned is the one in Jerusalem. ... (linuriyahu min ayātinā signifies that) it is indicative of the fact that along with the Holy Sanctuary of Mecca, the custodianship of Palestine and its sanctuary will also be given to the Ishmaelites. (Al-Bayan 3/62)

Third, in verse 59, Allah has made clear the reasoning behind not sending down additional signs to warn and threaten the disbelievers of Quraish. The reason, as told, is that whenever such signs were dispatched, rather than paying attention and becoming alarmed, people would reject them and ridicule them. For illustration, the text mentions the sign of the she-camel sent to the people of Thamud, and their subsequent denial of it.

Fourth, verse 60 continues in the same vein. It cites three instances of signs provided to the Quraish. These are the besiege of Mecca[8], the occurrence of the Night Journey (*Isra*), and the accursed tree[9]. The Qur'an details that the Quraish's reaction was no different than that of earlier communities—they too engaged in the worst behavior by denying and making fun of God's signs. As a result, these warnings did not foster faith and submission in them; rather, they only escalated their transgression.

Among the three signs outlined previously, the second instance involves Prophet Muhammad's (PBUH) journey to the Al-Aqsa Mosque. This indicated that the guardianship of both Mecca and the Sacred Mosque, as well as Palestine and the Al-Aqsa Mosque, was to be handed over to Prophet Muhammad (PBUH). The disbelievers of Quraish mocked it, transforming a significant warning and a threat into a *fitnah* (trial) for themselves. Javed Ahmed Ghamidi writes:

> *This is a reference to the incident of the night journey with which*

---

[8] It is a reference to the verses where the Almighty gave the glad tiding of closing in on Meccans from all sides. It was an explicit prediction of the fate the Quraish of Mecca had to meet at the conquest of Mecca. For more details, please read verse 41 of Surah al-Rad and the verse 44 of Surah al-Anbiya

[9] It refers to the Zaqqum tree mentioned in the Holy Qur'an. A note about this tree in al-Bayan reads:

> *The tree of zaqqūm, which neither gives shade nor fruit, is referred to here. It will be a heap of thorns which the dwellers of Hell will eat in distress. It will burn their bellies as if boiling water is circulating in them. It is because of these characteristics of this tree that it is called Mal'oona (accursed) by the Qur'an. In other words, God has not granted it with the benefits of flowers, fruits and shade. On the contrary, He has deprived it of all these things and thereby made it a symbol of His curse. When the Qur'an mentioned it to warn and frighten people, the miscreants of the Quraysh made it also a subject of making fun. They would mockingly say: Look at this person! On the one hand, he says that Hell will contain fire which will burn down stones and on the other hand, is informing us with the same tongue that trees also exist in this fire. (Al-Bayan, 3/94-95)*

the surah began. Since there was also a warning in it for both the Quraysh and the Israelites that besides the Sacred Mosque, the Bayt al-Maqdis too is now being entrusted to the Prophet (PBUH) it was made fun of. Mocking words like 'see now they are trying to forcibly occupy the Bayt al-Maqdis' were cracked. So much so that in the words of Imam Amin Ahsan Islahi, the thing that was meant to warn and admonish them and to inform them of the future became a trial for them because of their misdeeds. (Al-Bayan 3/94)

Fifthly, the word *ru'ya* is a very common and widely utilized term in Arabic. It corresponds to 'dream' in English, Hindi, and Urdu, implying the act of seeing something in one's sleep. It is widely used in poetry and prose to connote the meaning of dream. Its meaning is established as such in Arabic lexicons. It appears around seven hundred times in Hadith literature, carrying the same meaning. In the Holy Qur'an too, this term has been used seven times across chapters, and on every occasion, it implies nothing else than a dream. Given the usage and connotations of this term, it is imperative that in the mentioned verse it should be interpreted as a dream, thus, the journey of *Isra* ought to be regarded not as a corporeal expedition but as a spiritual experience.

Sixthly, however, the dream referred to here is not the mundane dream that is a regular experience for humans. It is not by means of that nature. Instead, this vision is a kind of divine revelation, exclusively accessible to the honored prophets. Ordinary people have no connection to it. What is revealed in this type of dreams to the prophets is true, aligns with reality, and is fact-based. Sometimes, these dreams are clearer and more vivid than what one sees with their eyes when awake. Imam Amin Ahsan Islahi discusses this type of vision:

...The dreams shown to the prophets, peace be upon them, are visions of truth. They have several distinctive characteristics. First, a true dream is one of the channels of divine revelation. Just as Allah Almighty conveys His guidance to His prophets and messengers in the form of words through an angel, in some

instances, He also communicates guidance through dreams.

The second characteristic is that this vision is exceedingly clear, unambiguous, and luminous like broad daylight (Ka-Falqi As-Subh), providing the prophet with complete satisfaction and tranquility of heart. Even if there are symbolic elements in the vision, Allah Almighty makes their interpretation clear to His prophet.

The third characteristic is that when the purpose is to show events and realities, this mode is more reassuring for a divine prophet because it allows for the full details of events to be observed, along with the representation of meanings and realities that are otherwise difficult to capture in words.

The fourth characteristic is that the insights gained through these dreams are more definitive, comprehensive, and thousands of times deeper and more extensive than what is seen with the naked eye. Eyes might be deceived, but a true dream is devoid of any deceit. The eyes can only see within a limited scope, but a dream can encompass a substantially wider range. Eyes are limited to observing only visible forms, whereas a dream grasps meanings, truths, and enlightenment as well. Prophet Moses, peace be upon him, desired to see the divine manifestation with his own eyes but found it unbearable. By contrast, through the visions shown to our Noble Prophet, peace be upon him, during the Night of Ascension, he observed all of them without his vision being overwhelmed. (Tadabbur-e-Qur'an 4/475-476)

From this explanation, it is clear that this was a formal journey, organized by the command of Allah Almighty, and during this journey, everything the Prophet (PBUH) observed was real, definitive, and certain.

Seventhly, the language and structure of the aforementioned verses from Surah Isra indicate the completion of the discussion. The Qur'an does not provide any further or related details about this matter elsewhere. Therefore, one must regard this as a distinct, unique, and complete event, and avoid trying to relate it to any other incident mentioned in the Qur'an and hadith literature.

~~~~~~~~~~

2. The Incident of *Qāba Qawsayn* (The distance of two bows)

وَالنَّجْمِ اِذَا هَوٰى . مَا ضَلَّ صَاحِبُكُمْ وَمَا غَوٰى . وَمَا يَنْطِقُ عَنِ الْهَوٰى . اِنْ هُوَ اِلَّا وَحْيٌ يُوْحٰى . عَلَّمَهٗ شَدِيْدُ الْقُوٰى . ذُوْ مِرَّةٍ ۛ فَاسْتَوٰى . وَهُوَ بِالْاُفُقِ الْاَعْلٰى . ثُمَّ دَنَا فَتَدَلّٰى . فَكَانَ قَابَ قَوْسَيْنِ اَوْ اَدْنٰى . فَاَوْحٰى اِلٰى عَبْدِهٖ مَآ اَوْحٰى . مَا كَذَبَ الْفُؤَادُ مَا رَاٰى . اَفَتُمٰرُوْنَهٗ عَلٰى مَا يَرٰى.

The stars, when they fall, bear witness that your companion is neither lost nor has he gone astray. He does not speak out of his own fancy. This [Qur'an] is but a revelation sent down to him. He has been taught by one mighty in power, towering in character and endued with wisdom. Thus, he appeared such that he was on the higher horizon. Then he drew near and bent down until he was within two bows' length or even closer. God then revealed to His servant that which He revealed. Whatever he saw was not his heart's delusion. Then will you now quarrel with him over what he is seeing with his eyes? (53:1-12)

Background

These verses from Surah Al-Najm were revealed to refute the allegations of fortune-telling that the Quraysh leaders leveled against Prophet Muhammad (PBUH). Whenever the Prophet (PBUH) would present the Qur'an to people, they would get captivated by its unique style, the inimitability of its language, and the sweetness of its articulation. Similarly, he used to share his experiences and observations about the revelations of the divine messages. Consequently, people were naturally drawn towards him. The Quraysh leaders could not endure seeing people pay attention to him and accepting his message as a divine

11

revelation. The only path to survival for them was to cast doubts on the words that flowed from him and the divine revelation. For this purpose, they started accusing him of being a poet or a madman, and even, God forbid, labeled him as a fortune-teller or an astrologer. They based their accusations on the premise that his recitations were metrical and rhyming, carried news of the unseen, and attributed the news to the angels. Clearly, these false claims were made in light of the actions of fortune-tellers and astrologers who would chant in rhythm and rhyme, predict the future, and ascribe their conjectures to jinn or astral entities.

The Noble Qur'an responded to these baseless allegations by addressing the Quraysh of Mecca and demolished their false allegations with logical arguments, delineating the following facts:

The first point of clarification was addressed to the people of Mecca, stating: 'Your companion (Muhammad) has not lost, nor deviated, implying that the one who is claiming prophethood among you has spent his life with you since birth. You know his character and history. You have always known him as truthful and trustworthy and have commended his virtues and integrity. Now, for declaring his prophethood, you accuse him of being a fortune-teller, God forbid, and claim he has lost his way or has strayed - this is a blatant accusation. Realize that he has not wandered from the truth; instead, he is firmly on the right path led by his Lord. It is you who are lost; despite knowing all, you reject his prophethood by deeming him a fortune-teller and an astrologer.'

The second argument exposed that, 'O Quraysh, the Qur'an that your companion recites to you originates not from his own thoughts or desires. It is a revelation meant to guide you. The Prophet receives it as divine inspiration, and he makes no modifications or additions to it.'

The third point made is that this teaching of revelation is conveyed by the noble and respected Angel Gabriel (AS). He is empowered with immense strength, possessing high attributes, extraordinary abilities, and competence. No one can intervene in his delivery or dare to corrupt it during the descent from heaven to earth. He is defined by his honesty and is both wise and knowledgeable. Owing to these attributes, he delivers the exact message, knowledge, and instructions to Allah's messenger as instructed by Allah the Almighty. He ensures the message remains unchanged. Neither angel, jinn, human, nor any other being in existence can intimidate or mislead him to err in this mission[10].

Imam Amin Ahsan Islahi writes:

> *...Every attribute and capability of that angel is exceedingly potent and resilient. There is absolutely no possibility that any other spirit influence or over-awe him or deceive or cause any confusion in the instruction of the book or that he himself commit any mistake or be afflicted with doubt or uncertainty. The Almighty has protected him from all such weaknesses so that he is able to discharge the responsibility entrusted to him with full honesty and sincerity. (Tadabbur-e-Qur'an 8/53-54)*

Details

The context of this event describes the incident of Gabriel's (RA) appearance before Prophet Muhammad (PBUH) in his true guise for the very first time. The details of the incident as inferred from the verses are as follows:

The event started with the appearance of Gabriel the Trustworthy on the highest horizon before the Prophet Muhammad (PBUH)[11]. The narrative style of the verse suggests that he revealed himself in his

---

[10] In Surah al-Takwīr (81), the Holy Qur'an describes Gabriel (AS) in the following words: *'That this indeed is the word brought by a noble messenger, endued with great power, held in very high honor before the Lord of the Throne. He is obeyed there and is also very trustworthy.'*

[11] It is the horizon's upper edge, which is directly above the Earth in a straight line, where the full moon appears with its entire brilliance on a moonlit night or where the sun rises at noon.

authentic guise[12], his complete stature[13], and Prophet Muhammad (PBUH) beheld him in entirety with his own eyes wide open while not asleep. Al-Bayan reads:

The actual words are: Al-Ufuq Al-A'la. It refers to the horizon which is directly in front of a person's line of sight. This is a mention of the first revelation and Gabriel's meeting with the Prophet (PBUH). The implication is that he appeared in a stark and unambiguous way the way the full moon or the midday sun appears and the Prophet (PBUH) saw him with his open eyes. (Al-Bayan 5/65)

Subsequently, Gabriel (AS) leaned towards the Prophet Muhammad (PBUH) who was on the earth. Meaning, he turned towards the Prophet (PBUH) with complete concentration, supreme regard, and absolute respect[14]. Javed Ahmed Ghamidi writes:

Then he drew near and bent down' This is a mention of the great attention and profound affection with which Gabriel (AS) taught the Prophet (PBUH) so that whatever guidance he is being given

---

[12] It was not his usual practice. Normally, he would visit the Prophet (PBUH) in human form or in some other form.

[13] Hadith reports reveal that his stature was such that it seemed as if he encompassed the entire sky, and he had more than six hundred wings.

[14] Imam Ahsan Islahi has explained this verse further in the following words:

It was not that he taught the Prophet (PBUH) from a distance without caring whether he had fully heard him or not and if he did, was able to understand it or not; on the contrary, with full attention and focus, he delivered the words in a manner that he be able to fully hear and understand them. Here it needs to be kept in mind that the knowledge provided by the devils of the soothsayers is mentioned in by the Qur'an as Khatifa Al-Khatfah, implying that it is a stolen piece of information which thieves and crooks have got hold of. Obviously, when the teachers are thieves, they would only be teaching their students the way thieves do. The Qur'an has here prominently mentioned the nature and method of teaching of Gabriel so that the difference in teaching of both is fully highlighted. (Tadabbur-e-Qur'an 8/54-55) was fully heard and was understood by him. (Al-Bayan 5/65)

Afterwards, Gabriel came so close to the Prophet Muhammad (PBUH) that only a small distance separated the two. Having approached this proximity, he conveyed to the Prophet (PBUH) the revelation he had brought from Allah[15]. Since the objective at this juncture in Surah An-Najm is to explain the nature and reality of the event, the details of the content of the revelation have not been elaborated upon.

From what has been recounted regarding the incident of *Qāba Qawsayn* (a distance of two bows' length), the following points are evident:

1. The Prophet Muhammad (PBUH) was not asleep.

2. He witnessed Gabriel (PBUH) emerging from a very elevated position in the sky.

3. Gabriel was in his real form.

4. He then came exceptionally close to the Prophet, so close that approximately the span of two bows' length remained between them.

5. He then imparted to the Prophet (PBUH) the part of the Qur'an which Allah had commissioned to him.

6. Prophet Muhammad (PBUH) observed the entire event fully awake and with his eyes open.

7. The details of the event and its context make it clear that this is a complete and self-contained occurrence, uniquely transpiring on its own. It bears no connection to any other event.

8. *Qāba Qawsayn* (the distance equivalent to two bows' length) is an Arabic term denoting extreme closeness.

Aspects not cited in the account include:

1. It is not specified where the Prophet Muhammad (PBUH) was

---

[15] However, since this incident is mentioned to argue for the authenticity of the Qur'an, the logical inference is that some part of the Qur'an alone was revealed on this occasion.

present at the time of this event.

2. There is no indication whether the event took place during the day or at night.

3. There is no detailed description of the revelation delivered to the Prophet Muhammad (PBUH).

Explanation

The salient points regarding the interpretation and explanation of the verses are as follows:

Firstly, the words *Fa-kāna qāba qawsayni aw adnā* have been mentioned to express the closeness and proximity of Gabriel to Prophet Muhammad (PBUH). This implies that he drew so close to the Prophet (PBUH) that the distance between the two was no more than the length of two bows or even less[16]. The aim here is not to determine the actual distance but to convey the extreme closeness. It is stated in Al-Bayan:

> *This simile is in accordance with the taste of the Arabs and occurs to describe extreme proximity and nearness. The 'Aw' here is referring to the fact that the purpose is to merely allude to the proximity; the purpose is not to mention the exact distance; it could have been more or less. (5/65)*

Secondly, in the words *Fa Awha Ilaa 'Abdihi Maa Awha* (God then revealed to His servant that which He revealed), it is clear that the subject of the verb *Fa Awha* is not Angel Gabriel, but Allah Almighty Himself. Since the original source and the originator of revelation is Allah Almighty, using an angel to deliver the revelation does not affect His status as the originator of the message[17]. The possessive pronoun

---

[16] This is the same style as the way we speak words of 'one or two yards' to describe limited distance.

[17] In 'So He revealed to His servant whatever He revealed,' the subject 'He revealed' might initially seem to refer to the Angel Gabriel. Based on this,

in *Abdihi* necessarily refers to Allah Almighty. Ascribing this pronoun to Gabriel implies polytheism (shirk), which is not permissible according to the Qur'an. The Qur'an and Sunnah categorically state that the status of deity is only and solely for Allah Almighty, hence servitude is solely related to Him.

Thirdly, to describe the nature of the incident, the words *Maa Kadhab Al-Fu'aadu Maa Raa'a. Afa Tumaaroonahu 'Alaa Maa Yaraa* (Whatever he saw was not his heart's delusion. Then will you now quarrel with him over what he is seeing with his eyes?) have been mentioned. These words make it completely clear that what Prophet Muhammad (PBUH) observed was in the state of wakefulness and with open eyes. It was neither a dream shown by Allah during sleep nor an allegory etched onto His heart and mind by Allah[18]. It was a physical observation made with all outward senses and full consciousness and cognition. Imam Amin Ahsan Islahi, in his commentary on this section of the Surah, writes:

> *This is an affirmation and approval from Allah Almighty regarding the Prophet's observation, so that no one should construe it as a figment of the heart or a deception of the soul. The incident is not a self-deception or illusion. The Prophet peace be upon him practically experienced this observation. ...He is only informing you about what his eyes see and what his ears hear. If these things are invisible to you, it does not negate reality. (Tadabbur-e-Qur'an 8/55-56)*

Fourthly, the incident of Qāba Qawsayn which is the appearance of Gabriel from the horizon and his coming very close to the Prophet Muhammad (PBUH) does not go beyond this description in these

---

some Sufis have derived the meaning that God, may He be exalted, has, God forbid, designated the Prophet Muhammad (PBUH) as the servant of Gabriel. This is an utterly false interpretation. If one considers the context and style of the Holy Qur'an, there is no room for such an interpretation.

[18] It should be noted that both of these instances, when they occurred with the Messenger of Allah (PBUH), were from Allah and were based on absolute truth.

verses. The words and style of the text indicate the completeness of the description. Furthermore, there is no additional or auxiliary detail mentioned anywhere else in the Qur'an regarding this incident. Therefore, it is obligatory to accept this as a specific, unique, and complete event and not to attempt to link any other Qur'anic and prophetic event to it.

Fifthly, in the mentioned verses of Surah Al-Najm, it is stated about the Gabriel (AS):

عَلَّمَهُ شَدِيدُ الْقُوٰى. ذُو مِرَّةٍ فَاسْتَوٰى. وَهُوَ بِالْاُفُقِ الْاَعْلٰى. ثُمَّ دَنَا فَتَدَلّٰى. فَكَانَ قَابَ قَوْسَيْنِ اَوْ اَدْنٰى.

He has been taught by one mighty in power, towering in character and endued with wisdom. Thus, he appeared such that he was on the higher horizon. Then he drew near and bent down until he was within two bows' length or even closer. (53:5-9)

Some scholars and commentators believe that these verses refer to Allah Almighty instead of Angel Gabriel. In our opinion, this is incorrect for several reasons.

Firstly, the phrases like *Dhu Mirratin Faistawa, Shadeedul Quwa,* and *Dāna fa-tadallā* are used in such a way that does not match the grace of the Lord of the Worlds. The style of describing abilities, attributes, and actions seems more appropriate for creatures than for Allah Almighty.

Secondly, when Gabriel's capabilities are mentioned in Surah Al-Takwir, a similar style is employed. Therefore, by the principle of *Al-Qur'an yufassiru ba'dahu ba'dan* (parts of the Qur'an explain its other parts), these words of the Surah also refer to Gabriel (AS). The Qur'anic text is as follows:

اِنَّهُ لَقَوْلُ رَسُولٍ كَرِيمٍ. ذِى قُوَّةٍ عِنْدَ ذِى الْعَرْشِ مَكِينٍ. مُطَاعٍ ثَمَّ اَمِينٍ.

That this indeed is the word brought by a noble messenger, endued with great power, held in very high honor before the Lord

of the Throne. He is obeyed there and is also very trustworthy.
(81:19-21)

Imam Amin Ahsan Islahi writes in his commentary on these words:

These verses describe the attributes of the angel Gabriel (AS) who
imparted this message to the Prophet, peace be upon him. He is
referred to as Shadeedul Quwa signifying that he possesses all
noble qualities and capabilities to the highest degree, and each of
his traits and capacities is exceedingly robust and steadfast. No
other being is capable of influencing or daunting him, of
betraying him, of causing any perplexity in his teachings, of
missing any detail, or of being swayed by any insinuation. The
Almighty Allah has safeguarded him against all such frailties
so that he can carry out the task assigned to him with utmost
sincerity and reliability, free from any corruption or disruption.
In Surah At-Takwir, this angel is commended as follows:
Innahu laqawlu rasūlin karīm. Dhī quwwatin 'inda dhī al-
'arshi makīn. Muṭā'in thamma amīn." Dhū mirratin,
implying that he is firm in both intellect and character,
incapable of being beguiled or bribing someone, or of being
bribed or swindled himself. This term connotes moral and
intellectual excellence. (Tadabbur-e-Qur'an 8/53-54)

Thirdly, the conclusion of the discussion on the introductory
paragraph of Surah Al-Najm ending with verse 18 makes it evident
that these observations, like all the others that have been mentioned,
pertain to the signs of Allah. They are not about the person of Allah
Himself. The Almighty says:

لَقَدْ رَاٰى مِنْ اٰيٰتِ رَبِّهِ الْكُبْرٰى.

He has seen his Lord's great signs.

Imam Amin Ahsan Islahi explains the verse in the following words:

This explicates the experiences of the Prophet (PBUH) during
this particular event. It has been stated that he witnessed some of
the magnificent signs of his Lord. No detailed description of the

19

signs has been provided as neither words suffice to describe them nor human intellect can grasp them. However, the use of the word Kubrā suggests that these signs were of a magnitude greater than those observable in the horizons and within oneself by any discerning person. ...Nevertheless, it is important to remember that the Prophet (PBUH) only saw the signs from his Lord, not the Almighty Allah in person . (Tadabbur-e-Qur'an 8/57)

~~~~~~~~~~

3. The Incident of *Sidrat al-Muntaha* (The sighting of Gabriel)

وَلَقَدْ رَاٰهُ نَزْلَةً اُخْرٰى. عِنْدَ سِدْرَةِ الْمُنْتَهٰى. عِنْدَهَا جَنَّةُ الْمَاْوٰى. اِذْ يَغْشَى

السِّدْرَةَ مَا يَغْشٰى. مَا زَاغَ الْبَصَرُ وَمَا طَغٰى. لَقَدْ رَاٰى مِنْ اٰيٰتِ رَبِّهِ الْكُبْرٰى.

And he has seen him once again descending near the farthest lote-tree, close to which is the Paradise of Repose, when the lote-tree was being covered with that which was covering it. His sight did not falter nor lost its poise. He has seen his Lord's great signs. (53:13-18)

Background

This incident is also recounted in Surah Al-Najm and is mentioned within the same context as the previously described incident, serving as a counterargument to the allegations of sorcery hurled by the Quraish chieftains against the Messenger of Allah (PBUH).

Details

After seeing Gabriel on the high horizon and at the distance of two bows (*Qāba Qawsayn*), the Messenger of Allah (PBUH), saw him again. The style of the conversation indicates that this second incident of sighting of Gabriel happened on a different occasion from the first; no additional encounters occurred in between.

The purpose of recounting this second sighting is to dispel any notion that the Prophet's earlier vision of Gabriel was an illusion or misconception—God forbid—since such clarity of sight also transpired on a subsequent occasion. Hence, there is no ground for doubt or uncertainty[19]. Javed Ahmed Ghamidi writes in his *Al-Bayan*:

> *This is a mention of the second meeting. It seems that after this, these meetings started to happen with great frequency and without any break. The implication is that this observation made by the Prophet (PBUH) did not take place just once so that people may regard it a flight of fancy or some misunderstanding. He also saw Gabriel again and at this instance too Gabriel was in his real form. (5/65-66)*

The Prophet (PBUH) observed Gabriel for the first time as he emerged from the higher horizon. When he saw him for the second time, he was close to *Sidrat al-Muntaha* (The Lote Tree at the Farthest Limit).

After the mention of *Jannat al-Ma'wa* (the Garden of Refuge), there is a reference to something overshadowing the *Sidrat al-Muntaha* (Lote Tree) without specifying any name or detail. This indicates that the Prophet (PBUH) witnessed a manifestation of divine light and glory in a form beyond the limits of language and expression, and beyond the comprehension of ordinary human understanding. The author of Al-Bayan writes:

> *This style shows that at that time such was the extent of divine disclosures and manifestations on the lote-tree that words are*

---

[19] Here, the question may arise whether the Prophet Muhammad, peace be upon him, saw Gabriel in his original form only twice. According to several hadith reports, the answer is affirmative. It is narrated in a Hadith from Sahih of Imam Muslim that Aisha (RA), said: The Prophet (PBUH) said: Gabriel, peace be upon him, is referred to in the mentioned verses of Surah At-Takwir and Surah Al-Najm. I saw him in his true form only on two occasions, the form in which Allah created him. I saw him descending from the sky, and his presence spanned from the sky to the earth. (Hadith No. 457)

unable to portray them. (5/66)

The state in which the Prophet's vision neither dazed nor crossed the limits has been described in the words *Mā Zāgha Al-Basaru Wa Mā Ṭaghā* (His sight did not falter nor lost its poise). This affirms that the Prophet saw it in state of wakefulness.. He saw with his very own eyes, in full wakefulness, what the Lord intended to show him. The glowing illuminations, bright lights, and visions of brilliance that were bestowed upon his sight were met with intense focus and deep immersion. On this very occasion, in spite of the boundless splendor and the blinding brightness, his vision remained steady and unflinching, fully engaged with the scenes before him. Al-Bayan notes:

...In spite of the great extent of divine disclosures, the sight of the Prophet (PBUH) was neither dazed nor crossed the limits; in fact, he saw them with full concentration, attention and assurance. (5/66-67)

On this profound occasion, the Prophet (PBUH) witnessed the sublime signs of his Lord. The phrase *Laqad ra'ā min āyāti rabbihi al-kubrā* (He has seen his Lord's great signs) signifies this event. Though no particular sign is individualized herein, the term *kubrā* (great) intimates that the signs he beheld were of such a magnitude that they surpass human knowledge and grasp. Al-Bayan elucidates:

No details are provided of these signs; hence neither is it possible for words to describe them nor can they be understood by our intellect and imagination. However, it is evident from the words of this verse that these signs were beyond the ones which we observe in the world within us and that around us. (5/67)

The conclusions that can be drawn from the above descriptions regarding the event at *Sidrat al-Muntaha* are:

1. The Prophet (PBUH) was fully awake.

2. He saw Gabriel (AS) descending from *Sidrat al-Muntaha*.

3. This was the second instance where the Prophet (PBUH) saw Gabriel (AS) in his true form.

4. This station was located beyond *Sidrat al-Muntaha* and before *Jannat al-Ma'wa*, serving as a juncture between the world of humanity (*'alam-e-nasoot*) and the divine realm (*'alam-e-lahoot*).

5. Apart from seeing Gabriel (AS), the Prophet also witnessed some extraordinary signs of Allah that defy human description and comprehension.

6. All these observations were made by the Prophet (PBUH) with eyes fully open and while completely awake.

7. In spite of the great extent of divine disclosures, the sight of the Prophet (PBUH) was neither dazed nor crossed the limits; in fact, he saw them with full concentration, attention and assurance.

The details not specified in the narrative include:

1. The exact location where the Prophet (PBUH) was at the time of this experience is not mentioned.

2. It does not detail whether this event took place during the day or at night.

3. Besides the station of *Sidrat al-Muntaha* and the presence of Gabriel (AS), it is not specified which other places and personalities the Prophet observed.

Explanation

The essential elements for interpretation and understanding of the verses are as follows:

Firstly, what is the nature *of Sidrat al-Muntaha*? Evidence from the Qur'an and Hadith indicate it is a point that represents the ultimate frontier of the tangible universe or the domain of existence, traversing the seven heavens. Beyond that lie the *Jannat al-Ma'wa*, and it is from there that the unseen realm commences, where the sovereign throne of the Lord of both worlds is situated. These two spheres are also referred to in our tradition as 'the realm of humanity' (*'alam-e-nasoot*) and 'the realm of divinity' (*'alam-e-lahoot*). Imam Amin Ahsan Islahi writes:

> *The place of the farthest lote-tree is the one where this world of ours ends. It seems that this lote-tree divides our world from the divine realm which is beyond our observation. Neither are we aware of the boundaries of these two worlds nor of the reality of this sign called the lote-tree which bifurcates the two. These things belong to the category of the mutashābihāt. Hence as per the directive of the Qur'an, it is essential to profess faith in them and one should not try to determine their real form and shape. Only God knows their real form. The knowledge of those who have sound knowledge increases through such things. People who make efforts to try to find out their real form and shape, falter and go astray. (Tadabbur-e-Qur'an 8/56)*

Secondly, the allusion to *Jannat al-Ma'wa* serves to elucidate the eminent status of *Sidrat al-Muntaha* and to designate its surroundings. It is evident from Surah As-Sajdah of the Qur'an that it is not the Paradise which individuals are promised as a reward for their faith and deeds. It denotes the gardens which serve as a preliminary sanctuary for the righteous ones prior to their entrance into the actual Paradise. The text articulates:

اَمَّا الَّذِيْنَ اٰمَنُوْا وَعَمِلُوا الصّٰلِحٰتِ فَلَهُمْ جَنّٰتُ الْمَاْوٰى نُزُلًا ۢ بِمَا كَانُوْا يَعْمَلُوْنَ.

Those who accepted faith and have done righteous deeds, for them are orchards of bliss as an initial hospitality in reward of their deeds[20]. (19:32)

Thirdly, concerning the site of *Jannat al-Ma'wa*, it apparently is located at the outset of the realm of divinity. Imam Amin Ahsan Islahi

---

[20] A footnote on this verse given in al-Bayan reads:

> *This is a mention of the orchards where the dwellers of Paradise will be kept before they enter it. It will be their foremost station of hospitality. The plural Jannātu is used for these orchards. This shows that each person will have his own orchard. (al-Bayan 4/102)*

remarks:

> *It seems that just as the Sidrat al-Muntaha stands at the terminal edge of the domain of humanity, 'Jannat al-Ma'wa likewise situates at the threshold of the domain of divinity. This recognition clarifies that the Prophet Muhammad (PBUH) encountered Gabriel (AS) the second time at the intersection where both domains converge. (Tadabbur-e-Qur'an 8/57)*

Fourthly, the incident at *Sidrat al-Muntaha*, namely the vision of Gabriel (AS) by the Prophet Muhammad (PBUH) with unshielded eyes and utter serenity at the locus of *Sidrat al-Muntaha*, is limited to as described in these verses. The verses *Wa laqad raahu nazlatan ukhra* (and he saw him another time by the *Sidrat al-Muntaha*) distinctly differentiate this occurrence from the event of *Qāba Qawsayn*. Additionally, the Qur'an does not furnish any further or supplemental details regarding this event. Consequently, it is essential to recognize it as a discrete, independent, and complete occurrence without amalgamating it with any other Qur'anic or Hadith depiction.

~~~~~~~~~~

4. The Event of *Shaq al-Sadr* (splitting of chest) and *Mi'raj*

عن شريك بن عبد الله أنه قال سمعت أنس بن مالك يقول: ليلة اسرى برسول الله صلى الله عليه وسلم من مسجد الكعبة انه جاءه ثلاثة نفر قبل ان يوحى إليه وهو نائم فى المسجد الحرام، فقال اولهم: ايهم هو؟ فقال اوسطهم: هو خيرهم، فقال آخرهم: خذوا خيرهم، فكانت تلك الليلة.

فلم يرهم حتى اتوه ليلةً اخرى فيما يرى قلبه، وتنام عينه، ـــــــ ولا ينام قلبه، وكذلك الانبياء تنام اعينهم ولا تنام قلوبهم، ـــــــ فلم يكلموه حتى احتملوه فوضعوه عند بئر زمزم، فتولاه منهم جبريل، فشق جبريل ما بين نحره إلى لبته حتى فرغ من صدره وجوفه، فغسله من ماء زمزم بيده

25

حتى انقى جوفه، ثم اتى بطست من ذهب تور فيه من ذهب محشوًّا إيمانًا وحكمةً، فحشا به صدره ولغاديده يعنى عروق حلقه ثم اطبقه.

ثم عرج به إلى السماء الدنيا، فضرب بابًا من ابوابها، فناداه اهل السماء من هذا؟ فقال جبريل: قالوا: ومن معك؟، قال: معى محمد، قال: وقد بعث؟، قال: نعم، قالوا: فمرحبًا به واهلاً، فيستبشر به اهل السماء لا يعلم اهل السماء بما يريد الله به فى الارض حتى يعلمهم.

فوجد فى السماء الدنيا آدم، فقال له جبريل: هذا ابوك آدم فسلم عليه، فسلم عليه ورد عليه آدم، وقال: مرحبًا واهلاً بابنى، نعم الابن انت فإذا هو فى السماء الدنيا بنهرين يطردان، فقال: ما هذان النهران يا جبريل؟، قال: هذا النيل والفرات عنصرهما، ثم مضى به فى السماء، فإذا هو بنهر آخر عليه قصر من لؤلؤ وزبرجد، فضرب يده، فإذا هو مسك اذفر، قال: ما هذا يا جبريل؟ قال: هذا الكوثر الذى خبا لك ربك.

ثم عرج به إلى السماء الثانية، فقالت الملائكة له مثل ما قالت له الاولى من هذا قال جبريل: قالوا ومن معك؟ قال محمد صلى الله عليه وسلم، قالوا: وقد بعث إليه؟ قال: نعم، قالوا: مرحبًا به واهلا .

ثم عرج به إلى السماء الثالثة، وقالوا له مثل ما قالت الاولى والثانية، ثم عرج به إلى الرابعة، فقالوا له مثل ذلك، ثم عرج به إلى السماء الخامسة، فقالوا مثل ذلك، ثم عرج به إلى السماء السادسة، فقالوا له مثل ذلك، ثم عرج به إلى السماء السابعة، فقالوا له مثل ذلك.

كل سماء فيها انبياء قد سماهم، فاوعيت منهم إدريس فى الثانية، وهارون فى الرابعة، وآخر فى الخامسة، لم احفظ اسمه، وإبراهيم فى السادسة، وموسى فى السابعة ‬‬‬‬ بتفضيل كلام الله ‬‬‬‬ فقال موسى: رب لم اظن ان يرفع على احد !

ثم علا به فوق ذلك بما لا يعلمه إلا الله، حتى جاء سدرة المنتهى، ودنا

للجبار رب العزة، فتدلى، حتى كان منه قاب قوسين او ادنى، فاوحى الله فيما اوحى إليه خمسين صلاةً على امتك كل يوم وليلة.

ثم هبط حتى بلغ موسى، فاحتبسه موسى، فقال: يا محمد، ماذا عهد إليك ربك؟ قال: عهد إلى خمسين صلاةً كل يوم وليلة، قال: إن امتك لا تستطيع ذلك فارجع، فليخفف عنك ربك وعنهم، فالتفت النبى صلى الله عليه وسلم إلى جبريل كانه يستشيره فى ذلك، فاشار إليه جبريل: ان نعم إن شئت فعلاً به إلى الجبار، فقال وهو مكانه: يا رب، خفف عنا فإن امتى لا تستطيع هذا، فوضع عنه عشر صلوات.

ثم رجع إلى موسى، فاحتبسه فلم يزل يردده موسى إلى ربه حتى صارت إلى خمس صلوات، ثم احتبسه موسى عند الخمس، فقال: يا محمد، والله لقد راودت بنى إسرائيل قومى على ادنى من هذا، فضعفوا فتركوه، فامتك اضعف اجسادًا وقلوبًا وابدانًا وابصارًا واسماعًا، فارجع، فليخفف عنك ربك كل ذلك يلتفت النبى صلى الله عليه وسلم إلى جبريل ليشير عليه ولا يكره ذلك جبريل، فرفعه عند الخامسة .

فقال: يا رب، إن امتى ضعفاء اجسادهم وقلوبهم واسماعهم وابصارهم وابدانهم، فخفف عنا، فقال الجبار: يا محمد، قال: لبيك وسعديك، قال: إنه لا يبدل القول لدى كما فرضته عليك فى ام الكتاب، قال: فكل حسنة بعشر امثالها فهى خمسون فى ام الكتاب وهى خمس عليك.

فرجع إلى موسى، فقال: كيف فعلت؟، فقال: خفف عنا اعطانا بكل حسنة عشر امثالها، قال موسى: قد والله راودت بنى إسرائيل على ادنى من ذلك، فتركوه ارجع إلى ربك فليخفف عنك ايضًا.

قال رسول الله صلى الله عليه وسلم: يا موسى، قد والله استحييت من ربى مما اختلفت إليه، قال: فاهبط باسم الله.

قال: واستيقظ وهو فى مسجد الحرام.

It is narrated from Shareek bin Abdullah. He says that he heard Anas bin Malik (RA) describe the night when the Prophet Muhammad (PBUH) was taken from the Masjid al-Kaaba. He narrates: Before the revelation began, the Prophet Muhammad (PBUH) was sleeping in the Sacred Mosque when three individuals (angels) came to him. One of them asked: 'Who among these (people) is he?' The one in the middle answered: 'He is the best among these (people).' The last one said: 'Take the best among them.' (Then the three returned). That was all that happened that night.

After that, the Prophet Muhammad (PBUH) did not see them until they came again on another night. At that time, his condition was such that his heart was seeing, but his eyes were sleeping, And his heart never slept. This is the case with all prophets; their eyes may sleep, but their hearts never sleep. They did not speak to him, but lifted him and laid him beside the well of Zamzam. Then, among them, Gabriel (AS) took him into his custody. Gabriel (AS) split open the part of his body from his throat to the lower part of his chest and took out whatever was inside his chest and abdomen. Then they washed him with Zamzam water using their hands until he was completely purified. Afterwards, a golden tray containing a golden bowl filled with faith and wisdom was brought. Gabriel (AS) filled his chest and the veins of his neck with it and then sealed the chest back as it was.

Then Gabriel (AS) took him on a flight towards the lowest heaven. Upon reaching, they knocked on one of its doors. From heaven, a voice asked: 'Who is it?' He replied: 'Gabriel.' The question came: 'Who is with you?' The answer was: 'Muhammad' Asked: 'Has he been invited?' Gabriel (AS) said: 'Yes.' They said: 'Welcome, he is very welcome. The inhabitants of the heavens are pleased with his arrival.' (However,) the inhabitants of the heavens do not know what Allah intends from them concerning the earth until they are informed about it.

Then, on this lowest heaven, he (Prophet Muhammad) saw Prophet Adam (PBUH). Gabriel (AS) said to the Prophet (PBUH): He is your father, greet him. Prophet Muhammad (PBUH) greeted Prophet Adam (PBUH), and he responded to the greeting. Then Adam (PBUH) said: 'Welcome, a good son and a good prophet.' Meanwhile, he saw two rivers flowing in the lowest heaven. He asked: 'Gabriel, what are these rivers?' Gabriel (AS) explained: 'These are the real forms of the Nile and the Euphrates.' Then Gabriel escorted him forward, and the Prophet (PBUH) saw another river at the banks of which there was a palace made of pearls and emeralds. When he put his hand into the river, he found its soil as fragrant as musk. He asked: 'Gabriel, what is this?' He said: 'This is Al-Kawthar, which your Lord has reserved especially for you.'

After that, Gabriel (AS) took him to the second heaven. There, the angels said the same thing as the angels of the first heaven had said. Hence, they asked who was with him. The answer was: 'Muhammad (PBUH) is with me.' They asked: 'Has he been invited?' Gabriel (PBUH) said: 'Yes.' They said: 'Welcome, he is very welcome.'

Then Gabriel (AS) took him to the third heaven, where the angels said the same thing as those before them had said. Then Gabriel (AS) took him to the fourth heaven, where the angels said the same thing as those before them had said. Then Gabriel (AS) took him to the fifth heaven, where the angels said the same thing as those before them had said. Then Gabriel (AS) took him to the sixth heaven, where the angels said the same thing as those before them had said. Then Gabriel (AS) took him to the seventh heaven, where the angels said the same thing as those before them had said.

On each heaven, prophets were present (with whom the Prophet Muhammad met). The names of these prophets were also mentioned. (The narrator mentions that) he remembered these names: Idris (PBUH) on the second heaven, Harun (PBUH) on the fourth heaven, another prophet on the fifth heaven - whose name he could not recall - Abraham (PBUH) on the sixth heaven, and Moses (PBUH) on the seventh heaven - because he had the honor of speaking directly with Allah. - Moses (PBUH), seeing the Prophet Muhammad (PBUH) accompanied by Gabriel (AS) and learning that he was being taken above the seventh heaven, exclaimed in astonishment: 'My Lord, I did not imagine that anyone would be raised above me!'

Then Gabriel (AS) took him above this (seventh heaven) to those heights known only to Allah until he reached Sidrat al-Muntaha. Then Allah descended and came close to him until there was only the distance of two bow lengths or even lesser between the two. Then Allah imparted His revelation to him and commanded him to pray fifty times in a day, which became obligatory for his Ummah.

Afterwards, he descended and reached Moses (PBUH). Moses (PBUH) stopped him. He asked: 'O Muhammad, what responsibility has Allah placed upon you?' He said: 'I have been commanded to pray fifty times in day and night.' Moses (PBUH) said: 'Your Ummah does not have the strength for this, (so my advice is) go back and ask for a reduction on behalf of yourself and your Ummah.' The Prophet Muhammad (PBUH) turned towards Gabriel (AS), as if seeking his advice. Gabriel (AS) indicated it was okay if he wished to return. Consequently, he returned to the same place in the presence of Allah (where he had met God earlier). Prophet Muhammad requested: 'O Lord, grant us concession in this matter, for my Ummah does not have the strength (to pray fifty times).' (Accepting the request) Allah reduced it by ten prayers (to make it forty prayers a day).

Upon return, when Prophet Muhammad (PBUH) reached Moses (PBUH), he stopped him again. (And gave the same advice, upon which Muhammad (PBUH) returned to the presence of Allah). The process of being sent back by Moses (PBUH) for a reduction continued (and Allah kept reducing it) until the number of obligatory prayers was reduced to five. Moses (PBUH) then stopped him again and (as usual) said: 'O Muhammad, by Allah, I tried to convince my people, Israelites, to accept even less than this, but they showed weakness and abandoned (the obligation). Your Ummah is even weaker in heart, body, and vision. So, go back once more so that Allah may further reduce it.' The Prophet Muhammad (PBUH) looked towards Gabriel (AS) to seek his opinion. Gabriel (AS) did not dislike this. Hence, he took him to the almighty Allah for the fifth time.

Prophet Muhammad (PBUH) requested: 'O Lord, the people of my Ummah are weak in heart, body, hearing, and vision, so I request further reduction.' Allah said, 'O Muhammad!' The Messenger of Allah said, 'Labbaik wa Sa'daik (I am at Your service, O Allah, I am at Your service).' Allah said, 'My decree does not change. (Thus, the command will remain) as I have decreed upon you in the Mother of the Book (i.e., the Lauh Mahfuz -Preserved Tablet). (However, the form of reduction for your nation will be that) one virtuous deed will be equal to ten virtuous deeds. Hence, in the Mother of the Book, these prayers remain fifty, but for you, their number will be five. (As if the reward of one prayer will be equal to ten prayers).'

(With this command) Prophet Muhammad (PBUH) returned to Moses (PBUH). He asked what happened. Prophet Muhammad replied that Allah had reduced the prayers in such a way that the reward for one (prayer) has been made equal to ten (prayers). In response , Prophet Moses (PBUH) repeated (the same advice) and said, 'By Allah, I had demanded even less from my people, the Israelites, but they showed weakness and abandoned (the obligation). Go back once more so that Allah may reduce it further.'

The Messenger of Allah (PBUH) said, 'Moses, by Allah, I now feel ashamed to go back to my Lord for the same purpose.' Moses (PBUH) then said, 'Well, then, descend in the name of Allah.'

Anas ibn Malik (RA) narrates that after this, when (Prophet Muhammad) woke up, he was in the Masjid al-Haram. (Sahih Bukhari, Kitab al-Tawhid, No. 7517)

Background

This incident is the fourth and the last of the series. It is narrated by Anas bin Malik (RA) and documented by Imam Bukhari in his Sahih. The incident comprises two parts. The first part details the opening of the chest (*Shaq al-Sadr*), in which Gabriel (AS) split the noble chest of Prophet Muhammad (PBUH), cleansed it with Zamzam water, and filled it with faith and wisdom before closing it . The second part relates to the ascension (*Mi'raj*), whereby the Messenger of Allah (PBUH), escorted by Gabriel (AS) the trustworthy, ascended toward the heavens, traveled through the seven heavens and the *Sidrat al-Muntaha*, got ushered into the Divine Presence of Allah, and returned with the gift of prayers.

This event is far from a common human experience. It is associated with prophethood. When Allah Almighty selects a person for this position, He endows him with the honor of His direct conversation and communication. This communication can manifest in diverse manners, as ordained by the divine wisdom and will of Allah. This process has been explained in *Meezan* in the following words:

Prophethood denotes the choosing of an individual for divine communication. It implies that when Allah Almighty selects a person for this office, He engages in direct communication with him. The Qur'an has apprised us that humans have traditionally received this privilege in two forms:

One is through a direct conversation which transpires behind a veil. The individual hears a voice yet the originator remains unseen. This is what Moses (PBUH) experienced. He abruptly heard a voice emanating from a tree at the base of Mount Sinai, but the speaker remained concealed from his sight.

The second method is the revelation. Through revelation, Allah instills something into a person's heart. It can happen in two ways: First, Allah places His words directly into the heart of a prophet. Second, He sends an angel to impart His message into the prophet's heart on His behalf. This can occur in both states of consciousness—while asleep and while awake. The message received sometimes takes a symbolic form in dreams. The circumstances under which the Prophet Muhammad (PBUH) received revelation are reported in hadith reports, indicating that the revelation could start with a sound similar to a bell ringing. It would be so intense that even in cold weather, the Prophet (PBUH) would perspire profusely. What is the essence of this reality? The Qur'an indicates that it is something beyond human comprehension. Hence, it is stated:

وَيَسْـَٔلُوْنَكَ عَنِ الرُّوْحِ ۖ قُلِ الرُّوْحُ مِنْ اَمْرِ رَبِّيْ وَمَآ اُوْتِيْتُمْ مِّنَ الْعِلْمِ اِلَّا قَلِيْلًا

They ask you about the rūḥ [that is being revealed to you]. Tell them: This rūḥ is a directive of my Lord and you have been given very little knowledge of such facts. (Qur'an 17:85) (Meezan 130-131)

Some of the most significant methods Allah used to communicate with the prophets, as detailed above, are as follows:

1. Direct communication while remaining unseen.

2. Imparting God's words into the prophet's heart

3. Sending His message through an angel to the prophet during his wakefulness

4. Presenting realities in symbolic form to the prophet when he is awake

5. Sending His message through an angel in the prophet's dreams

6. Presenting realities in symbolic form in dreams

The narrative about the event of *Mi'raj* (Ascension) confirms that the last two methods were used.

Details

The event of *Mi'raj* as described in the hadith narrative is as follows:

1. One night, the Prophet Muhammad (PBUH) was sleeping in Masjid al-Haram. The word used by the narrator are *Wahuwa nā'imun fī al-Masjid al-Harām* (he was sleeping in the Sacred Mosque). Some other people were also sleeping there[21].

2. While sleeping, he saw that three angels arrived and recognized him[22]. That night, the angels went back after seeing him asleep.

3. They arrived again on another night[23]. They found the Prophet (PBUH) sleeping in the Sacred Mosque again. It is evident from the words *Yarā qalbuhu, wa tanāmu 'aynu* (his eyes were asleep but his heart was awake).

4. They lifted his sacred body and brought it to the well of Zamzam. There, Gabriel (AS) opened his chest and cleansed his heart with Zamzam water. A golden bowl filled with wisdom and knowledge was brought; Gabriel (AS) took the wisdom and knowledge from the bowl[24] and put it into his chest. Afterwards, they closed his chest[25].

5. Once this process was finished, Gabriel (AS), the trustworthy, guided the Prophet (PBUH) through the heavens. He traveled

---

[21] The following interaction among the angels supports this assumption: 'Who among these (people) is he?' The one in the middle answered: 'He is the best among these (people).' The last one said: 'Take the best among them.'

[22] They probably intended to ensure that when they come to take him for the coming Night of Ascension, they make no mistake in recognizing him.

[23] The hadith report does not specify whether they arrived the very next night or a few nights later.

[24] The style of the conversation indicates that intangible things like wisdom and knowledge were shown to him symbolically in form of a physical object.

[25] All these occurrences happened in the realm of a dream because it has already been in the beginning of the hadith that the eyes of the Prophet were asleep when the incident occurred.

upwards, meeting a prophet at each of the seven heavens. As remembered by the narrators, the Prophet met Adam (PBUH), Idris (PBUH), Aaron (PBUH), Moses (PBUH), and Abraham (PBUH). In the second heaven, He also saw earthly rivers of Euphrates and Tigris and the Celestial Pond of Kawthar, depicted symbolically as three streams.

6. After ascending through the seven heavens, the Prophet (PBUH) was taken to *Sidrat al-Muntaha*. Near this location, he achieved a proximity to the Divine Presence, akin to the closeness of the two ends of a bow. There, Allah Almighty revealed the commandment of fifty daily prayers.

7. When the Prophet (PBUH) was returning from his journey with the directive, he once again met Prophet Moses (PBUH) on the seventh heaven. Moses asked him about the covenant with Allah. The Prophet informed him of the obligation to perform fifty prayers. Moses, drawing upon the experience with his own people, suggested that performing fifty prayers a day would be difficult for his *Ummah* (community). It would therefore be appropriate for him to return to the Divine Court and request a reduction in the number of prayers. The Prophet (PBUH) found the suggestion reasonable, so he returned to the Divine Presence and requested a reduction in the number of prayers. Allah Almighty accepted the request and granted a concession of ten prayers. Upon returning, he met Prophet Moses (PBUH) again, who repeated the same advice. The Prophet (PBUH) went back to Allah's Presence and obtained further concessions of ten prayers again.. This process of requesting reductions continued until only five prayers remained. With utmost generosity, Allah Almighty declared each prayer equal to ten prayers and informed the Prophet (PBUH) that the fifty prayers would remain as they are in *Umm al-Kitab* (the Mother of the Book), but only five prayers would be obligatory for his Ummah. Thus, when his people perform five prayers, they will be counted as fifty.

8. After this, Prophet Moses (PBUH) advised further reductions even in the five prayers, but this time, the Prophet (PBUH) did not accept his suggestion. Afterwards, he returned to Masjid al-Haram with the gift of five prayers.

Explanation

The important points of clarification and explanation of the hadith are as follows:

Firstly, the Prophet's (PBUH) journey and all the events and observations occurred in the world of dream. The introductory and final words of the hadith explicitly clarify this nature. The opening statement reads:

> *They arrived another night to see that the Prophet's eyes were sleeping but his heart was not. This is the case of the prophets that even when they sleep, their eyes sleep but their hearts stay awake.*

The closing words are:

> *when (the Prophet) woke up, he was in the Masjid al-Haram*

Secondly, to describe proximity to the Divine Being, the phrase *Hattā kāna minhu qāba qawsayni aw adnā* has been used. These are almost the same words used in Surah Al-Najm to convey the closeness of Gabriel (AS) to the Prophet (PBUH), as it states: *Fa-kāna qāba qawsayni aw adnā*. In the Arabic language, such metaphorical phrases are akin to expressions in our language like 'a distance of a yard or two' or 'a gap of a few hand-lengths,'[26] which are used to convey the idea of closeness or proximity between locations or objects. Thus, it is plausible to assume that the narrative borrowed the style of expression from Surah Al-Najm to emphasize the Prophet's (PBUH) nearness to Allah.

---

[26] This well-known verse attributed to Qa'im Chandpuri is as follows:

'Qismat ki khoobi dekhiye, tooti kahan kamand'

'Behold the irony of fate—where the rope of ambition broke.'

Thirdly, based on the mentioned style of expressing divine proximity, it is highly likely that the Prophet (PBUH) had the honor of beholding Allah Almighty. Some other hadith narratives also ascribe the following statement to the Prophet (PBUH): 'I saw my Lord in the most sublime form.' It is evidently clear that this refers to seeing in the world of dream. The reason is that the words of the narrative *Wa tanāmu 'aynuhu, wa lā yanāmu qalbuhu* (His eyes sleep, but his heart remains awake) indicate that the incident of *Mi'raj* occurred when the Prophet's (PBUH) eyes were asleep but his heart was not. It is also narrated in some other hadith narratives that the Prophet (PBUH) saw Allah Almighty in the world of dreams while the Prophet (PBUH) was sleeping. Here is one such hadith narrative[27]:

عن معاذ بن جبل رضى الله عنه، قال: احتبس عنا رسول الله صلى الله عليه وسلم ذات غداة عن صلاة الصبح حتى كدنا نتراءى عين الشمس، فخرج سريعًا فثوب بالصلاة فصلى رسول الله صلى الله عليه وسلم وتجوز فى صلاته، فلما سلم دعا بصوته، فقال لنا: على مصافكم كما انتم، ثم انفتل إلينا، ثم قال: اما إنى ساحدثكم ما حبسنى عنكم الغداة.

انى قمت من الليل فتوضات وصليت ما قدر لى، فنعست فى صلاتى حتى استثقلت فإذا انا بربى تبارك وتعالى فى احسن صورة.

فقال: يا محمد، قلت: لبيك رب، قال: فيم يختصم الملا الاعلى؟ قلت: لا ادرى، قالها ثلاثًا.

قال: فرايته وضع كفه بين كتفى حتى وجدت برد انامله بين ثدىى، فتجلى لى كل شىء وعرفت.

Mu'adh bin Jabal said: God's Messenger was detained one morning from observing the prayer with us (because he had not arrived to lead the congregation) till the sun had almost appeared over the horizon. He then came out quickly and led the

---

[27] A detailed discussion on this issue has been provided in an upcoming section titled 'The Concept of Seeing Allah Almighty'

37

congregation. He conducted the prayer in a shortened form (because of shortage of time); then when he had given the salutation, he called out to us saying, 'Keep to your rows as you were.' Then turning to us he said, 'I shall tell you what detained me from you this morning. I got up during the night, performed ablution, and prayed what I could; but during my prayer I dozed and was overcome, and there and then I saw my Lord in the most beautiful form.' He addressed me by name, and when I replied, 'At Thy service, my Lord,' He asked, 'What do the angels near My presence dispute about?' and I replied that I did not know. He asked it three times. Then I saw Him put the palm of His hand between my shoulder-blades, so that I experienced the coolness of His fingers between my nipples so everything became clear to me and I attained knowledge. (Tirmidhi No. 3235)

Fourthly, the words *Fahiya khamsūna fī Ummil-Kitāb wa hiya khamsun 'alayka* indicate that the obligation of the five daily prayers was established at this particular event. This view is also the common position among our scholars. However, this position does not align with the Qur'an and certain hadith narratives, as prayer has been a fundamental aspect of Allah's religion from the beginning. The Qur'an clearly states that prayer was the main duty enjoined upon the noble prophets by Allah Almighty. A Hadith from Sunan Abi Dawud, No. 393, reinforces this perspective, where it is stated that once Gabriel the Trusted informed the Messenger of Allah (PBUH) that prayers have always been performed five times a day. Therefore, the most probable assumption from this perspective is that the obligation of prayer commenced with the prophethood of Prophet Muhammad (PBUH), and that during the *Mi'raj*, the background realities of this duty may have been symbolically presented to him.

~~~~~~~~~~~~~

Summary

The above pages provided a detailed description of the stance of our esteemed teacher, Javed Ahmed Ghamidi on the issue. The prominent points of the discussion are:

- The events described under the title '*Isra* and *Mi'raj*' are not one but four different occurrences.

- These comprise the *Isra*, the *Qāba Qawsayn*, the *Sidrat al-Muntaha*, and lastly, the *Mi'raj*.

- The first three events are referred to in the Qur'an, while the last is mentioned in the hadiths.

- The specific timings and sequences of these events are not clearly stated in the Qur'an or the hadiths.

- Of these, two happened in the realm of the dreams and the other two are based on conscious observations.

- All these events are divine in nature, specific to prophethood, and are synonymous to divine revelation.

- It makes no difference to their veracity whether these observations occurred in dreams or in a state of consciousness. The difference of sleep or wakefulness does not affect their credibility.

- Events described in the Qur'an are beyond any doubt or uncertainty, but those conveyed through hadith narratives, if reliably traced back to the Prophet (PBUH), must also be accepted unreservedly.

- No Muslim is permitted to deny these occurrences or to diminish their divine status by comparing them with ordinary human experiences.

- The texts describing these four events clearly emphasize their unique nature.

- However, some narrators in the Hadith literature have presented them as a single event, leading to scholars and commentators treating them as such in their descriptions.

- This conflation may have happened due to textual similarities, narrative overlaps, memory issues, misunderstandings, or descriptive flaws.

- Misunderstandings can be prevented by interpreting the hadith reports in the light of the Qur'an instead of the other way around.

Chapter Two

Traditional Position and Its Critical Review

The traditional understanding of the events related to *Isra* and *Mi'raj* has been summarized in the Introduction section and may be referred to there for review. The significant academic points are as follows:

- The events of *Isra* and *Mi'raj* have been mentioned in both the Qur'an and hadiths. The Qur'an provides a brief description whereas the hadiths provide detailed accounts of the events.

- When the relevant passages from the Qur'an and Hadiths are combined, a cohesive story emerges that suggests it may be more logical to view it as a single event.

- The Prophet (PBUH) underwent this experience in full conscience and wakefulness, and witnessed the signs of Allah with both his physical sight and spiritual insight.

- It is true that the Qur'an and hadiths do not verbally affirm that the ascent was physical and the journey occurred while awake. However, the style of conversation in both the Qur'an and hadith indicate that it was a physical ascension and the journey took place in complete wakefulness.

- It is also true that the Qur'an has described the incident as *ru'ya*, which is commonly understood to mean seeing in a dream, i.e., a vision during sleep. However, interpreting it as a dream renders it a common occurrence and strips away its miraculous nature. Furthermore, such an interpretation affects the significance of the styles used in the Qur'an and Hadith which highlight the power and greatness of Allah in relation to this event. Therefore, it is necessary to interpret the word *ru'ya* in a context other than its common meaning, and use it in the sense of seeing while awake. Since Arabic literature contains several precedents of this style, it is entirely consistent with the language to use the word *ru'ya* to describe practical sighting (in state of wakefulness). Some hadith narratives claim that the event occurred in a spiritual form in the realm of dreams, but when we see them in context of and comparison to their text and chain of narrators of other hadith narratives, the position supporting a physical journey in complete wakefulness appears stronger.

- It also cannot be denied that the hadiths describing *Isra* and *Mi'raj* carry some contradictions — for example, there are differences in the descriptions of the observations, events described by the narrators, the numbers associated with the event, and in the chronological and spatial sequence of the events. Some aspects even seem to contradict the text of the Glorious Qur'an[28]. However, keeping the miraculous aspect of the event in mind, reconciling the various narrations, resolving the conflicts between statements, and rejecting the parts that contradict the Qur'an makes it entirely possible to establish a coherent narrative of these events. Thereafter, this emerges as a faith-inspiring miracle of the Messenger of Allah (PBUH) and a momentous event in the history of humanity.

In relation to these points, a study of some excerpts from highly reputed scholars will help understand the argument more deeply.

The author of Tafsir Ibn Kathir writes:

> *After considering all the Hadiths, including Sahih, Hasan, and Daeef ones, it is clear that there is consensus on the event of the Prophet Muhammad's (PBUH) journey from Mecca to Jerusalem. It is true that there are differences in the narrations and variations in the details, but such errors are possible because no one is free from mistakes except the Prophets.*

---

[28] For example, some narrators mention direct sighting of Allah Almighty. Most of the scholars consider this against the Holy Qur'an.

Regarding the differing accounts of whether milk and honey, milk and wine, or milk and water were presented to the Prophet Muhammad (PBUH), or all four, some narrations state that this happened in Jerusalem, while others say it occurred in the heavens. However, it is possible that these items were offered as hospitality at both places.

Furthermore, there is a debate on whether the Isra (night journey) happened with both the body and soul of the Prophet Muhammad (PBUH) or just the soul. Both views exist. Most scholars believe that the event occurred with both the body and soul while the Prophet was awake, meaning he was not sleeping. However, they do not dismiss the possibility that the event might have first been shown to him in a dream and then later occurred in reality. This is because the dreams of the Prophet Muhammad (PBUH) were as clear as daylight.

Allah Almighty has said: The dream We showed you We made it a trial[29] too for these people [because of this attitude of theirs].

Abdullah ibn Abbas (RA) explains in his commentary on Surah Al-Isra, verse 60, that 'vision' here refers to what the Prophet Muhammad (PBUH) saw with his eyes on the night he was taken on the journey. The 'accursed tree' mentioned is the Tree of Zaqqum (Bukhari, Hadith 4716). In this context, Allah Himself states, 'The sight [of the Prophet] did not swerve, nor did it transgress [its limit][30],' indicating that the vision was a function of his complete being, not just his soul.

Maulana Syed Abul A'la Maududi writes:

The Mi'raj event is mentioned both in the Qur'an and in Hadith. The Qur'an tells us why Mi'raj took place and what instructions God gave to His Messenger. The Hadith tells us how Mi'raj happened and what events occurred during this journey.

---

[29] Surah Al-Isra 17:60
[30] Surah Al-Najm 53:17

Details of this event have reached us through 28 contemporary narrators. Seven of the narrators were present during the time of Mi'raj, and 21 others later heard the story directly from the blessed tongue of the Prophet (PBUH). Different reports shed light on different aspects of the story, and when combined, they form a travelog, a more captivating, meaningful and enlightening one than any other found in the entire history of human literature. (Travelog of Mi'raj 3)

In Maulana Maududi's *Tafheem al-Qur'an*, he explains the verse of Isra as follows:

What was the nature of this journey? Did it take place in a state of sleep or in wakefulness? And did the Prophet (PBUH) physically embark on this journey, or was it merely a spiritual experience while he remained seated in his place? These questions are answered by the words of the Glorious Qur'an itself. The beginning with the words 'Subhāna alladhī asra...' indicates that this was a great supernatural event that happened by the infinite power of Allah. It is clear that for someone to see such things in a dream or in a state of unveiling is not significant enough to necessitate an introduction declaring the purity of the Being who enabled the vision or revelation. The words 'One night He took His servant...' clearly indicate a physical journey. These words do not fit for a dream journey or an unveiled spiritual journey. Therefore, we have no option but to accept that this was not merely a spiritual experience but a physical journey and a direct observation that Allah Almighty had His Prophet (PBUH) undertake. (2/589)

Mufti Muhammad Shafi has stated:

The journey from Masjid al-Haram to Masjid Al-Aqsa, which is mentioned in this verse, is known as Isra, and the journey from there to the heavens is known as Mi'raj. Isra is confirmed by explicit text in this verse (Surah Al-Isra 17:1), and the events of Mi'raj are mentioned in the verses of Surah Al-Najm and are established by mutawatir (successive) hadith reports... It is discerned from the commands of the Glorious Qur'an and the mutawatir hadiths, as detailed later, that the entire experience of Isra and Mi'raj was not just spiritual but was also physical, akin to the manner in which ordinary humans travel... When the Prophet, may the peace and blessings of Allah be upon him, revealed this event to the people, the disbelievers of Mecca rejected it and mocked the Prophet to the extent that some of the new Muslims renounced their faith upon hearing about it. If the incident was simply a dream, then why would such reactions occur? And this does not rule out the possibility that the Prophet may have experienced a spiritual Mi'raj in the form of a dream before or after this physical journey. The majority of the Ummah holds the view that the 'ru'yā' referred to in the Qur'anic verse 'Wa mā ja'alnā al-ru'yā allatī araynāka' implies actual seeing, but it is described as a 'ru'yā' to convey that it was like something seen in a dream. And if the word 'ru'yā' is literally interpreted as 'dream', it is not improbable to think that, in addition to the physical Mi'raj, there was a spiritual journey through a dream either before or after the event. Therefore, the reports by Abdullah ibn Abbas (RA) and Aisha, the mother of believers (RA), regarding the Mi'raj being a dream are accurate in their respective contexts. However, this does not mean there wasn't also a physical Mi'raj. (Maarif al-Qur'an 5/438-439)

Pir Karam Shah al-Azhari writes in his commentary, *Zia ul Qur'an*:

The word 'Subhān' indicates that Allah Almighty is devoid of all imperfections, deficiencies, and incapabilities. Such a claim necessitates evidence, for a claim without proof is unsubstantiated. As proof, the verse alladhī asra bi 'abdihi is cited because Allah is the one who made His beloved servant travel a vast distance within a fraction of the night and showed him significant signs and manifest evidence. A Being capable of shortening such a lengthy journey indeed possesses limitless power and supreme magnificence, and His nobility is free from any weakness or incapacity. Therefore, the event Allah has presented as evidence of His exaltedness cannot be an ordinary occurrence but must be one of the most significant, graceful, and astonishing events... .

The style of conversation in the Qur'an clearly explicates that this event was not a dream but happened in a conscious state. One may argue that another verse of the Holy Qur'an specifies it as a vision, meaning a dream. God Almighty asserts: Wa mā ja'alnā al-ru'yā allatī araynāka illā fitnatan lilnās. In this instance, the term ru'ya has been used, denoting a dream... When the Holy Qur'an has expressly pronounced it a dream, how could it be challenged?

In defense, it is necessary to articulate that most commentators believe that this verse does not refer to the event of Mi'raj, but to a different dream. And if someone insists that this verse specifically refers to the Mi'raj, then Ibn Abbas's following explanation dispels any ambiguity. He asserted: 'Here, vision pertains to seeing with one's eyes while awake...'

People also base their argument on a hadith reported by Anas (RA). According to his report, after describing the Mi'raj, the Prophet (PBUH) said: 'Then I woke up and found myself in Masjid al-Haram.' Regarding this hadith, the explanation of the hadith experts can suffice to resolve any misunderstandings automatically. Allama Alusi states that Sharik narrated these words from Anas. Sharik, the narrator, is not a good memorizer of hadith according to the experts of hadith... Allama Ibn Kathir claims that this report is one of the mistakes committed by Sharik. (2/626-627)

Hafiz Salahuddin Yusuf, a famous representative of the Ahle Hadith school of thought writes:

...This event is narrated by more than twenty-four Companions. In this regard, it holds the status of tawatur ma'nawi (mass transmitted by meaning). Therefore, certain or specific interpretations of some narrators cannot cast doubt on the entire event and its important details, nor can they be allowed to affect the miraculous nature of the event by declaring it as a dream.

Similarly, the opinion of some scholars that there were multiple occurrences of the Ascension (Mi'raj) based on differences in hadith narrator's views is not correct, nor is it a proper solution to the differences among the narrators. When a significant and dignified event is narrated by multiple people, minor discrepancies in the details of the event or occasional additions and omissions are not unlikely. It is common for such differences to appear in the accounts of multiple narrators. In such situations, one cannot deny the occurrence of the event or explain them as several events. Instead, one has to accept the event and its necessary details in light of the common points and components of diverse statements of narrators. (The Event of Mi'raj and its Observations 28-29)

He further writes:

These narrations come from different narrators; therefore, some of the details described in them vary as we have indicated earlier. When different people describe the details of a great event, such discrepancies are generally expected. Therefore, if some differences and misconceptions are found in the narrations about Isra and Mi'raj, it does not affect the soundness of the event in terms of its reliability. Scholars and interpreters of Hadith literature have clarified these discrepancies and misconceptions and have provided solutions and reconciliations where it was possible, after which the principal event becomes clear of all doubts. (The Event of Mi'raj and its Observations 42).

Hafiz Salahuddin Yusuf writes about the word *al-ru'ya* in verse 60 of Surah Al-Isra:

In the Glorious Qur'an, ru'ya is used in the sense of sighting only. Some people, referring to the following verse of the Qur'an, consider it to mean a dream: Wa mā ja'alnā al-ru'yā allatī araynāka illā fitnatan lilnās (And the vision We showed you was only a trial for the people.)

However, in this verse, ru'ya does not mean 'dream,' as it is often used. Here, it is used in the sense of actually seeing with the eyes, as this usage also exists in the Arabic language, so it is said: ra'aytuhuBi'aynay ru'yatan wa ru'yā (I saw him with my own eyes). Meaning, seeing with the eyes can be expressed with both words ru'ya and 'ru'yatan.' And Imam Jamaluddin Al-Qasimi, may Allah have mercy on him, writes: "In language, ru'ya is also used in the absolute sense of 'seeing' (ru'yah), and this is its real meaning... like (qurbī and qurbatan) are. (The Event of Mi'raj and its Observations 23)

Dr. Muhammad Luqman Salafi, a student of Sheikh Abdul Aziz bin Baz, summarizes the views of the early and later scholars on the nature and condition of the *Mi'raj* event in his Tafsir *Taysir al-Rahman*. He writes:

The majority view of the early and later scholars is that the Prophet (PBUH) went to Jerusalem and then to the heavens with both his body and soul. This is the opinion of Ibn Abbas, Jabir, Anas, Hudhayfah, Umar, Abu Huraira, Malik bin Sasaa, Abu Habba al-Badri, Ibn Mas'ud, Dahhak, Said bin Jubair, Qatadah, Said bin Al-Musayyib, Ibn Shihab, Ibn Zaid, Hasan, Masrooq, Mujahid, Ikrimah, and Ibn Jurayj (may Allah be pleased with them all). This is also the shared opinion of Tabari, Ahmad bin Hanbal, and most later jurists and hadith scholars, as well as scholastics and commentators.

Another opinion is that the Mi'raj was purely spiritual. Those who hold this opinion draw evidence from verse 60 of this surah: Wa mā ja'alnā al-ru'yā allatī araynāka illā fitnatan lilnās, arguing that the Qur'an has explicitly stated that it was a dream. Ibn Ishaq has reported from Aisha (RA), and Muawiya (RA) that the blessed body of the Messenger of Allah was not found missing from his sleeping place. And the Messenger of Allah (PBUH), himself said: 'While I was asleep,' indicating that during the event he was sleeping.

The third opinion is that the journey to Jerusalem was accomplished physically, and from there the spiritual journey took place toward the heavens. This is because the verse limits the night journey (Isra) to Masjid Al-Aqsa.

Qadi Iyad writes in his book 'al-Shifa' that the correct and true belief, Insha'Allah, is that the event of Ascension (Mi'raj) took place with both the body and soul of the Prophet (PBUH). The noble verse, authentic hadiths, and thoughtful consideration affirm this fact. Interpretational technique is used only when accepting the apparent meaning becomes impossible.

I hope the above details sufficiently explain the arguments upon which the traditional viewpoint is based. In the following pages, a critical review of these arguments will be offered in light of the stance of Javed Ahmed Ghamidi.

<center>~~~~~~~~~~</center>

Fundamental Principles of Discourse and Argumentation

Before presenting a critique of the traditional stance, we will outline the foundational principles upon which the argumentation of Javed Ahmed Ghamidi is based. His stance on *Isra* and *Mi'raj*, as mentioned in the previous pages, follows these principles. In the upcoming pages, these same principles will be the basis of argumentation for the understanding of his stance and the critique of the traditional stance. These are a few foundational principles of reason and tradition, without which attaining a correct understanding of religion and Shariah is not possible. They are as follows:

First, the Holy Qur'an holds the status of a scale and criterion in the religion[31]. This means that the Qur'an has a decisive status in all matters pertaining to religion. Thus, every statement, every claim, and

---

[31] It is God Who has revealed this Book of His with the decisive truth and [in this way in order to distinguish good and evil] sent down His scale. (42:17)
Very exalted and benevolent is the being who has revealed this Furqān to His servant so that it can warn the people of the world. (25:1)

every opinion from hadith and relics, history and biography, jurisprudence and interpretation will be weighed in its scale and tested against its criterion. Only that which it accepts will be accepted. That which it rejects will not be accepted as part of religion or its explanation and interpretation.

To act upon this principle, it is essential that hadith be understood in the light of the Qur'an, and anything that conflicts with the Qur'an and Sunnah should not be accepted. Javed Ahmed Ghamidi writes in his *Meezan*:

> ...*In religion, the Qur'an's status is that of a scale and a criterion. It oversees everything and has been sent down to distinguish between truth and falsehood, thus this matter does not require further argumentation that anything which contradicts the Qur'an must necessarily be rejected... The definitive and conclusive source of history regarding anything done by the Prophet (PBUH) with his position of prophethood and messengership is also the Qur'an.*
>
> *Hence, most of the contents of hadith are related to it as branches are to their origin and as commentary is to the text. To understand the explanations and derivations without looking at the original text is clearly impossible. If we analyze closely the mistakes made in understanding hadith thus far, this reality becomes plainly apparent. Incidents of stoning during the prophet's era, the killing of Ka'ab bin Ashraf, narrations about the punishment of the grave and intercession, and commands like 'Umirtu an uqātila-n-nās[32]' and 'Man baddala dīnahu faqtulūhu[33]' became the cause of confusion because they were not understood by relating them to their origins. (63-65)*

Second, the Holy Qur'an has been revealed in a clear Arabic language. Its words and idioms are free from ambiguity, vagueness, anomalies,

---

[32]Bukhari, No. 25; Muslim, No. 129: I have been commanded to fight against people.

[33]Bukhari, No. 3017: Kill those who change their religion.

and oddities It presents its message with complete clarity, which does not pose any difficulties for scholars to comprehend. *Meezan* reads:

> *The Qur'an has been revealed not just in Arabic, but in clear Arabic. This means in a language that is extremely distinct, devoid of any ambiguity; each word is clear and each style is familiar to its audience. It is stated: The Trusted Spirit has brought it down to your heart so that you also become a warner like other prophets, in very lucid Arabic. (Qur'an 26:192-195) In the form of a Qur'an that is in Arabic in which there is no flaw so that they can be secure from God's torment. (Qur'an 39:28)*
>
> *This is a clear fact about the Qur'an. Accepting it leads to the inevitable conclusion that no word or style in the Qur'an can be anomalous in terms of its meaning. It has been revealed using commonly known words and expressions to its audience. From the linguistic perspective, it contains no element of strangeness, but is clear and obvious in all aspects. Therefore, it must be translated and interpreted keeping in mind only the well-known meanings of its words. Any interpretation beyond these accepted meanings cannot be accepted under any circumstances. (20-21)*

In our view, most misunderstandings in traditional schools of thought occur because of ignoring the principles of reasoning and transmitted knowledge. These principles[34] have been blatantly ignored while trying to understand and decipher the events of *Isra* and *Mi'raj* . The texts of the Qur'an, which are definite in both proof and interpretation (*qati al-thaboot and qati al-dalalah*), were relegated to secondary importance, while the Hadith texts, which are speculative in proof and interpretation (*zanni al-thaboot and zanni al-dalalah*), were considered primary. Rather than interpreting hadiths in light of the Qur'an, the Qur'an has been interpreted in the light of hadiths.

---

[34] There is no doubt that the scholars of both the past and present accept these principles and also mention them in their foundational arguments. However, this acceptance and acknowledgment largely remain confined to the theoretical domain. In practice and in their application, these principles are often disregarded or overlooked.

The same occurred with the commonly known words and styles of the Arabic language, which were given rare and foreign meanings, deviating from their general application. This incorrect approach to knowledge and comprehension, and this reversal in the order of understanding and reasoning, have undermined the position of the Qur'an as criterion (*Furqān*) and scale (*Meezān*), neglected the established rules of language and expression, and relayed a message that contradicts the purposes of the Qur'an and Hadith in some aspects.

To comprehend what has transpired in this issue, a quick review of the relevant texts and the derived inferences will suffice. Anyone who reflects deeply will realize that various accounts have been merged to form an event, and then the verses of the Qur'an have been interpreted based on that constructed event. If a Qur'anic verse does not support the prearranged event, it is interpreted in a way that clashes with the common practice and language of the Qur'an. Similarly, if a narrative presents something discordant with the imagined event, it is disregarded, even if it complies with the standards of authenticity set by renowned Hadith scholars.

Single Incident or Four Separate Incidents?

From our traditional perspective, the detailed account of *Isra and Mi'raj* is generally perceived as a single event. Various references to the event in the Noble Qur'an and varying hadith narratives are declared as components of that same event. The necessary outcome of this approach is that all the evidence concerning reason and revelation, language and expression, as well as time and space, are treated as parts of a unified whole. Hence, the evidence for one aspect is cited in support of another, and so forth. Even if language, expression, context, and general application do not support these connections, people still insist on declaring them a chain of the same sequence. Any evidence indicating difference or contradiction is dismissed. For instance, Surah Al-Najm mentions that Prophet

Muhammad (PBUH) saw Gabriel (AS) with his own eyes at *Sidrat al-Muntaha*, while Surah Al-Isra narrates that the Prophet's journey to Al-Aqsa mosque occurred in a dream. The first instance denotes an awakened state of consciousness and the second indicates a vision, that is, a prophetic dream. Clearly, these two states are opposite and unique from one another. Now, if both these instances are taken to describe the same event simultaneously, then inevitably, the wording of one will need to be misinterpreted. That is, if this event is to be viewed as a visual experience, then the words *Ra'ā* (he saw) and *Mā zāgha-l-basaru wa mā taghā* (his sight did not swerve, nor did it transgress) would have to be explained in the context of a dream and slumber, and if it is to be understood as an event of wakefulness, then *ru'yā* (dream) would have to be interpreted as visual perception, that is, seeing with the eyes.

Consider that the Qur'an and hadith outline several events relating to Prophet Muhammad (PBUH). In some instances, it is one event, but its components and related issues are described in various places. There is also the case where the same setting is used to describe more than one event and then there are distinct incidents, each occurring separately and narrated at different occasions. The first case can be exemplified by the story of Adam and Iblis. The second case is represented by verses 59-60 of Surah Al-Isra, which pertain to three separate events. The last case illustrates events such as the encounter between Prophet Moses and Khidr (peace be upon them) or the duel between Prophet Moses and the magicians.

Now the question is, how can we determine whether a particular verse, hadith, narrative, or statement pertains to a single event, a unique event in itself, or multiple events? One possible answer might be to deduce this via intellectual effort, using one's imaginative capacity to piece together various disparate elements into a cohesive whole. Such an approach may be deemed acceptable when crafting a work of fiction, but holds no place in the discourse of understanding the contents of the Qur'an and Hadith or assembling the biography of Prophet Muhammad (PBUH). In these domains, the final and authoritative weight is given to those accounts or declarations that have reached us through unequivocal or acknowledged sources. If they amalgamate distinct incidents into a single event, then it shall be treated as one; otherwise, they must be viewed as individual occurrences. No attempt will be made to link them to one another through speculative interpretation.

If this concept is clear, it can then be easily understood that the attempt to merge four distinct events into a single incident is the fundamental misunderstanding that has made it difficult to comprehend the true nature and essence of these magnificent occurrences.

In our opinion, the compelling evidence that distinguishes these four events lies in the fact that their respective accounts do not depict them as a singular occurrence. The arrangement within their respective contexts, the choice of words, stylistic nuances, and their intended meanings and ends, all emphasize their distinctiveness. Hence, when the texts do not aggregate them into a single incident but rather depict them as separate happenings, then one is not entitled to merge them based upon personal interpretation, and portray them as a singular event.

If it is objected that these events do not explicitly state that they are distinct occurrences, such an objection itself demonstrates a lack of understanding of linguistic and rhetorical nuances. In the Qur'an, hadith, and accounts of *Seerah* and biographies, dates are generally not mentioned, nor is it explicitly stated that one event is directly connected to another, or that certain parts of an event precede or follow others. It is the narration of the event itself that determines whether it should be considered a standalone occurrence or as part of another event's sequence, either preceding or succeeding it. In such matters, the decisive authority rests with the speaker and their speech. It is they who determine whether a statement is definitive or ambiguous, detailed or concise, related or unrelated. The role of the listener or reader is merely to hear or read the text and strive to understand it. For this purpose, they rely on the use of words, sentence composition, customary language usage, context, and other similar indications to deduce the intent of the speaker. In the realms of explanation and interpretation, their duty is solely to elucidate the meaning contained within the text and the implied intent behind it. To go beyond this is akin to encroaching upon the speaker's domain—a violation for which neither religion, morality, nor scholarly reasoning offers any justification.

Apart from the principal argument, there are additional points to consider:

1. Difference in Locations

The journey of *Isra* is described in Surah Al-Isra, whereas the narratives of *Mi'raj* are found within the hadith. The incidents of *Qāba Qawsayn* and *Sidrat al-Muntaha* are recounted in Surah Al-Najm. Though the last two events are mentioned in Surah Al-Najm, the Qur'an distinctly distinguishes them as separate occurrences.

2. Difference in States

The experiences of *Isra* and *Mi'raj* transpired in dreams , while the encounters at *Sidra al-Muntaha* and *Qāba Qawsayn* took place during wakefulness. These distinct states are explicitly outlined within the textual sources.

3. Difference in Observations

The event of *Isra* involved observing earthly locations while remaining on Earth. The event of *Mi'raj* involved ascending to the heavens and observing celestial locations. The event of *Qāba Qawsayn* involved observing Gabriel (AS) on the higher horizon while still on Earth. The event of *Sidrat al-Muntaha* involved observing *Sidrat al-Muntaha* and the celestial lights and radiance while remaining on Earth.

4. Difference in Objectives

The purpose of the event of *Isra* was to announce the decision of entrusting both Masjid Al-Aqsa and Masjid Al-Haram to Prophet Muhammad (PBUH). The purpose of the event of *Mi'raj* was to exhibit the signs of God in the form of specific prophecy. The significance of the events of *Qāba Qawsayn* and *Sidrat al-Muntaha* was to make the Quraysh understand the truth and authenticity of the Qur'an.

5. Difference in Details

Each of the four events contains entirely distinct and unique details, making them separate and individual occurrences.

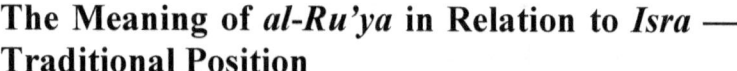

The Meaning of *al-Ru'ya* in Relation to *Isra* — Traditional Position

The event of *Isra* is mentioned in the noble Qur'an in Surah Al-Isra. Its opening verse depicts the journey from Masjid Al-Haram to Masjid Al-Aqsa, and in verse 60 the manner of this journey is discussed. It is commanded:

سُبْحْنَ الَّذِى اَسْرٰى بِعَبْدِهِ لَيْلًا مِّنَ الْمَسْجِدِ الْحَرَامِ اِلَى الْمَسْجِدِ الْاَقْصَا الَّذِى بَرَكْنَا حَوْلَهُ لِنُرِيَهُ مِنْ اٰيٰتِنَا اِنَّهُ هُوَ السَّمِيْعُ الْبَصِيْرُ

Flawless is the being who one night took His servant from the Sacred Mosque to that Distant Mosque whose surroundings We have blessed so that We can make him observe some of Our signs. Indeed, only He hears and knows all. (Qur'an 17:1)

... وَمَا جَعَلْنَا الرُّءْيَا الَّتِى اَرَيْنٰكَ اِلَّا فِتْنَةً لِّلنَّاسِ ...

...The dream We showed you We made it a trial too for these people [because of this attitude of theirs][35]... (Qur'an 17:60)

In relation to these verses, there is a consensus about two points:

Firstly, only the journey from Masjid Al-Haram to Masjid Al-Aqsa is described in Surah Al-Isra. The ascent to the heavens is not covered here.

Secondly, the term *al-ru'ya* that appears in verse 60 is connected to the same event of journeying to Al-Aqsa which is cited in the first

---

[35] It should be noted that verse 60 does not primarily aim to explain the situation of the event. It is only implied secondarily from the meaning of the text.

verse.

The recognized authority on the exegeses of the companions, their followers, and the followers of their followers, Imam Ibn Jarir al-Tabari states that there is a consensus among the leading exegetes that the term *ru'ya* in verse 60 refers to the night of Isra. This is noted in Tafsir Ibn Kathir:

> ... *Therefore, Imam Ibn Jarir adopted the stance that (this point in verse 60) refers to the night of Isra. ...In his view, the eminent scholars of exegesis are in agreement on this matter.* (5/85)

Imam Abu Abdullah Al-Qurtubi writes under verse 60 in his exegesis *Al-Jami' li Ahkam al-Qur'an*:

> *Allah Almighty says: 'The dream We showed you We made it a trial too for these people [because of this attitude of theirs].' In this verse, when the Almighty says that the purpose of the revelation of the Qur'anic verses is to warn and threaten, it refers to the verse describing the Isra event. The verse appears at the beginning of the Surah.* (10/282)

It is clear that both early and later scholars are in agreement that the mention of *al-ru'ya allatī araynāka* (the vision which We showed you) in verse 60 of Surah Al-Isra refers to the *Isra* event, and this is the same event highlighted in verse 1 of the Surah. This signifies that it is the unanimous opinion of scholars that the event of *Isra* took place in the world of dreams.

Ru'ya is a commonly employed word in the Arabic language and generally signifies seeing in a dream, just as we use *Sapna* in Hindi, and *Khwab* in Urdu. Arabic dictionaries list its meanings accordingly. In poetry and literature, the term is used to denote the concept of dreams. It appears approximately seven hundred times in the Hadith literature, invariably with the meaning of dream. The noble Qur'an also uses it in various Surahs a total of seven times, each instance conveying the notion of a dream.

Our scholars acknowledge its typical use in the context of dreams; in fact, they utilize this term when expounding on and translating the Qur'an and hadith to imply the idea of dreams. However, because they view the journey of *Isra* as a physical one, they interpret the *ru'ya* associated with this journey not as a dream but as a vision experienced while awake. Thus, according to them, the Prophet's journey was corporeal. Throughout this journey, the sights presented by God were perceived in a conscious state, and the Prophet (PBUH) witnessed them with his own eyes and clear sight.

The summary of the evidence upon which the scholars' stance is based is as follows. These are the very arguments that are presented to refute the position of Javed Ahmed Ghamidi on this subject.

1. The word *ru'ya* is most commonly utilized in the context of dreams. However, it is not solely confined to this implication. It is also used to denote seeing with open eyes. For example, the famous Arab poet Al-Mutanabbi has employed this word in one of his poetic verses not in the sense of viewing during sleep, but in a wakeful state. Therefore, deducing the meaning of direct sight from the term *ru'ya* within the context of Surah Al-Isra and interpreting the journey to Masjid Al-Aqsa as a physical venture aligns entirely with Arabic language and literature. Imam Ibn Hajar Al-'Asqalani has indicated in *Fath al-Bari* relating to the verse of Isra:

> *Among those who consider al-ru'ya to imply seeing in wakefulness include Mutanabbi, a famous poet. He writes: Your sight (ru'yaka) is sweeter than slumber for my eyes. (5/673)*

Similarly, the statement from the well-known Arab poet Al-Ra'i stands as: *Fa kabbara lil ru'ya wa hashsha fu-adihi* (He witnessed the *ru'ya* (scene) and shouted 'Allahu Akbar', with his heart leaping for joy.) This elucidates that in Arabic, the term *ru'ya* also encompasses the concept of seeing in an alert state.

2. The esteemed status of Abdullah ibn Abbas (RA) in terms of authenticating from the Arabic language and literature, and his explanations and interpretations of the Qur'an and hadith, is widely recognized. In Sahih Bukhari, it is reported from him that the term *ru'ya* in Surah Al-Isra refers to *ru'yatu 'ayn*, which means to see with one's own eyes[36]. If such an eminent commentator has given this interpretation, then there is no place for any more guesswork. His statement should be considered conclusive evidence on this topic. The author of Tafsir Ibn Kathir writes:

> *Abdullah Ibn Abbas (interpreting verse 60 of Surah Bani Israel) says that in this verse, the word 'al-ru'ya' implies seeing with open eyes that happened on that night when the Prophet was taken (to Masjid Al-Aqsa) (5/84)*

3. Having established that *ru'ya* also means to see with open eyes, and since the reputable scholar Abdullah Ibn Abbas (RA) has indicated this, it is imperative that the explanation of verse 60 should be guided by the context of verse 1. It would be incorrect to interpret the specifics of verse 1 from the stance of verse 60. The verbs, nouns, and expressions used in verse 1 are more indicative of a physical episode rather than a visionary one. Thus, the definition of *ru'ya* should be based on these considerations.

4. Before detailing the event in verse 1 of Surah Al-Isra, Allah Almighty described His purification from all flaws. The phrase *Subhāna alladhī* (Exalted is He) is employed for this purpose. The prerequisite of this mode of expression is that it should be succeeded by the description of a remarkably unique incident. If the event is perceived as a mere dream, the link between *Subhāna alladhī* for exalting Allah and the subsequent narrative weakens. This is because in dreams, long journeys or witnessing things against ordinary norms is a routine occurrence for humans. Such conditions in an event cannot be deemed astonishing or metaphysical to the listener. Therefore, the usage of *Subhāna alladhī* suggests that the subsequent event must be comprehended as a phenomenal miracle, showcasing Allah's power in an exceptional way. Evidently, this extraordinary aspect is accentuated when a trek of forty days is accomplished within a few hours of a single night.

---

[36] Bukhari, No. 4716

Imam Ibn Kathir writes:

> *A proof of this conclusion is the word 'Subhāna alladhī' (God describing His exaltedness). The start of the conversation with such an exceptional phrase indicates that a highly important event is going to be discussed. If we consider the event as an experience in a dream, such observations in dreams are not of much significance (5/40).*

5. The expression *Alladhī Asra bi 'abdihi* is mentioned in verse 1 of Surah Al-Isra, translated as "He who took His servant..." In this context, the verb *asra* does not imply a dream. Its significance is to physically transport. This is an activity that is exclusively associated with a physical existence. Thus, applying it to a dream would be inaccurate. Furthermore, the term *abd* (servant) cannot refer solely to the spirit, for *abd* signifies the amalgamation of soul and body. Therefore, the deployment of this term indicates that a physical entity, representing a fusion of soul and body, is contemplated. In Tafsir Ibn Kathir, it is mentioned:

> *Here, the words asra bi abdihi laylan have been used. The word 'abd' refers to the combination of body and soul (5/41).*

6. In verse 60, the incident is portrayed by the phrase *fitnatan lilnās* (trial for the people), elucidating that this episode was set forth as a trial for humankind. A fitnah or trial, by its nature, can only result from something extraordinary. In dreams, people frequently observe unusual things. When they share such observations with one another, it does not cause surprise or astonishment for anyone. People typically listen to others' dreams and share their own without any sense of amazement. A dream neither creates hesitation nor becomes a test or trial for them. If this is the general behavior of people, how is it possible that the Prophet (PBUH) narrated a dream, and it became a trial for them? This trial could only arise if the event were presented as a physical occurrence. In such a case, all the factors necessary for it to become a test would naturally be present.

Imam Ibn Hajar al-Asqalani states:

It is not permissible to dispute the fact that the journey to Al-Aqsa mosque in one night was undertaken in a state of wakefulness, because the apparent meaning of the Qur'an clearly affirms this. Additionally, the Quraysh rejected this claim, and if the journey to Bayt al-Maqdis had occurred in a dream, the Quraysh would not have denied it. (Fath al-Bari 1/460)

Maulana Syed Abul A'la Maududi provides a more thorough discussion on this subject. In his commentary on verse 60, he states:

The reference here pertains to the event of Mi'raj. The term 'ru'ya' in this context does not signify 'dream' as related to sleep; it implies seeing with one's own eyes. Clearly, if the event were merely a dream and the Prophet Muhammad (PBUH) had depicted it as such to the disbelievers, there would be no grounds for it to become a point of contention for them. People often have unusual dreams and share them, yet such dreams do not provoke astonishment to the extent that the teller would be ridiculed, accused of lying, or labeled as a mad. (Tafheem al-Qur'an 2/627)

7. It is narrated that when the story of the *Isra* event was told, people refused to believe it. The disbelievers derided it, and some Muslims even renounced their faith. This response from the people suggests that the journey was of a physical nature because had it been a dream, it would have simply been disregarded as a commonplace happening. Neither would the disbelievers have dismissed it, nor would there have been cases of Muslims abandoning their faith.

In Tafsir Ibn Kathir, it is expressed:

(The words of glory present the evidence that the event of Isra took place physically) Glorifying Allah requires that it must precede a highly important and graceful incident. However, taking the event as an experience in a dream cannot make the event an extraordinary one (and does not match the glorification). It is because in that case, neither the Quraish would hurry in rejecting the claim nor some Muslims would renounce their faith. (5/40)

Our scholars, based on these proofs, firmly state that to interpret the Prophet Muhammad's (PBUH) journey as a spiritual one or a dream is incorrect; it should be taken as a literal physical journey.

According to the esteemed teacher, Javed Ahmed Ghamidi, the scholars' position regarding the event of *Isra* is not correct. While acknowledging their scholarly stature and religious sincerity, the fact remains that their position contradicts the established principles of language and expression, the definitive foundations of reasoning, and the precedents set by the Qur'an and hadith. As a result, it amounts to attributing their own interpretation to the words of Allah and His Messenger (PBUH).

The details concerning the components and nature of the event of *Isra* have already been discussed earlier. Here, we will present the critique of the scholars' position as outlined by the esteemed teacher.

〰〰〰〰〰

Conclusive Evidence in the Debate over Physical or Spiritual Journey

The question arises whether the texts present such definitive evidence concerning the physical or spiritual nature of the *Isra* event as to decisively resolve the argument? The answer to this question is in the affirmative. The evidence lies in the fact that Allah has not left this matter ambiguous but has explicitly clarified the state in which this event occurred.

To understand this, when we examine the inaugural verse of Surah Al-Isra, we learn that the Prophet Muhammad (PBUH) was taken overnight from Masjid al-Haram to Masjid Al-Aqsa. This phrasing leaves open both interpretations. It could be perceived as a corporeal ascension while awake, or as a journey within a dream[37]. Were the

---

[37] The possibility of dreams arises because it is accepted based on the Qur'an, Hadith, and previous divine scriptures that dreams were one of the means of revelation. God would also show truths to His prophets in the state of sleep.

situation limited to only verse 1, relying on words such as *subhān*, *asra*, and *abd* for indicative or conjectural evidence might serve as the focal point[38], with one of the two interpretations then validated accordingly. However, the conversation extends beyond verse 1. Verse 60 introduces another element, and in it, the Word of Allah makes it clear that the event occurred within a world of vision.

This indicates that after the explicit declaration of Allah Almighty, a definitive and pivotal evidence has now come forth. As a result, the following points are its inevitable implications:

1. The term *al-ru'ya* will assume the role of the primary evidence, and all other proofs will become secondary.

2. The definition and interpretation of *al-ru'ya* will be determined in alignment with the standard usage in the Arabic language.

3. Since *ru'ya* in Arabic typically refers to seeing in sleep or a dream, the event will be deemed spiritual rather than physical, rendering all other potential interpretations invalid.

4. Interpretations of indicative evidence such as *subhān*, *asra*, and *abd* mentioned in verse 1 of Surah Al-Isra will likewise be considered in light of the definition and interpretation of *al-ru'ya*[39].

5. The term *ru'ya* will also be decisive concerning its relationship between the event of *Isra* mentioned in Surah Al-Isra and the incidents of *Sidrat al-Muntaha* and *Qāba Qawsayn* mentioned in Surah Al-Najm. As a result, it will be necessary to consider these as separate events because it has been explicitly mentioned that one occurred in the realm of dream

---

[38] It is conjectural (*zanni*) because these are not definitive in terms of being understood as wakefulness. For instance, the words *Ra'ā* (he saw) and *Mā zāgha-l-basaru wa mā taghā* (his sight did not swerve, nor did it transgress) in Surah Al-Najm are definitive in the sense of wakefulness.

[39] Meaning, it will not be the case that the definitive argument of the word *ru'ya* (dream) will be determined in light of these indicative arguments.

and it is clear regarding the other two that they took place in a state of wakefulness with open eyes. Thus, verse 60 of Surah Al-Isra holds the decisive position in distinguishing between verse 1 of the same surah and the relevant verses of Surah al-Najm. It establishes the basis for differentiating between the two contexts.

6. All the Hadiths and reports related to the event of *Isra* will be understood in the light of this definitive evidence, and anything that contradicts this will be declared against the Qur'an and hence rejected.

This explanation makes it clear that the term *al-ru'ya* serves as definitive evidence. It decisively refutes all the arguments that are commonly used as a basis in this matter, and which have been mentioned earlier in references such as Fath al-Bari, Tafsir Ibn Kathir, and other sources. Similarly, it is also sufficient to counter the arguments related to language and expression that are often presented in this discussion and have been adopted by the majority of scholars, both past and present.

With this being established, the argumentation of the esteemed teacher becomes complete in its entirety. After this, there is no need to scrutinize the mentioned arguments of the scholars individually and to demonstrate how they contradict the texts of the Qur'an and hadith, and the established facts of language and expression. However, since the early generations of Muslims (salaf) have presented these, the later generations have insisted upon them, and the general masses have accepted them, it seems necessary to comment on them. This commentary is included in the following pages. It should be regarded as a secondary consideration, and while reviewing it, the aforementioned primary argument should not be overlooked.

~~~~~~~~~~~~~~~

1. Meaning and Concept of *al-Ru'ya*

Ru'ya is a very common word in the Arabic language, used in the sense of dream. This meaning has been adopted in the Qur'an, hadith, literature, and dictionaries. Here are a few examples to illustrate this:

Arabic Lexicons

First, let's take a look at references from the mother of lexicons. In *al-Sihah fi al-Lugha* by Ismail bin Hammad al-Jawhari, it is written:

> *Al-ru'ya means something that a person observes in his or her dreams (6/2349)*

The well-known lexicon *Lisan al-Arab* by Ibn Manzur states:

> *Al-ru'ya is something that you see in your dreams. (8/278)*

In *Taj al-Arus* by al-Murtada al-Zabidi, it is quoted:

> *Al-ru'ya is something that you see in your dreams. (17/436)*

The statement in *Al-Mu'jam al-Waseet* says:

> *Al-ru'ya is something observed in dreams. (1/320)*

Imam Raghib Asfahani, in his renowned book *Mufradat al-Qur'an*, has ascribed the meaning of *ru'ya* to dreams seen in sleep. Moreover, he did not mention any other meanings. Furthermore, among the verses of the Holy Qur'an he has cited as evidence, there is the aforementioned verse of Surah Al-Isra. He writes:

> *Ru'ya means something that is seen in sleep. In a hadith, it is stated that 'Only ru'ya remain from prophethood.' In the Qur'an, it is mentioned that 'Allah showed His Messenger a true dream[40].' Additionally, it says, 'The dream We showed you, We made it a test for the people[41].' (209)*

These are just a few references from lexicons. In addition to these, every Arabic dictionary lists the meaning of the word *ru'ya* as seeing or dreaming in sleep. These can be found under the Arabic root *'ra'a'* in lexicons.

---

[40] Surah Al-Fath 48:27
[41] Surah Al-Isra 17:60

The Holy Qur'an

Next, look at the Holy Qur'an. The term appears in various places 7 times and on each occasion, it is used in the well-known and commonly used sense of a dream. Excluding Surah Al-Isra, the exegetes have translated it as a dream in all other instances. Note that of these six instances, four pertain to the dreams of prophets. All these instances are as follows, and under each is a note derived from Tafsir Ibn Kathir to give readers an idea of how explicit this term is in the context of a dream:

a. *The ru'ya of the Prophet Muhammad (PBUH) in Surah Al-Fath*

لَقَدْ صَدَقَ اللهُ رَسُوْلَهُ الرُّؤْيَا بِالْحَقِّ لَتَدْخُلُنَّ الْمَسْجِدَ الْحَرَامَ اِنْ شَآءَ اللهُ اٰمِنِيْنَ مُحَلِّقِيْنَ رُءُوْسَكُمْ وَمُقَصِّرِيْنَ لَا تَخَافُوْنَ...

Indeed, Allah affirmed His Messenger's dream (al-ru'ya) in truth: 'You will definitely enter the Sacred Mosque, if Allah wills, in security, [heads] shaved or hair cut short, not fearing [anyone]...' (48:27)

According to all exegetes, here *ru'ya* means a dream. For example, in *Tafsir Ibn Kathir*, it is mentioned:

The Messenger of Allah (PBUH) saw in his sleep (i.e., in a dream) that he went to Mecca and performed Tawaf of the Kaaba. He mentioned this to his companions while still in Medina. In the year of Hudaybiyyah, when he set out with the intention of performing Umrah, the companions were fully confident that they would see the fulfillment of this dream during this journey. (7/331)

b. *The ru'ya of Prophet Abraham (PBUH) in Surah As-Saffat*

فَلَمَّآ اَسْلَمَا وَتَلَّهُ لِلْجَبِيْنِ . وَنَادَيْنٰهُ اَنْ يّٰاِبْرٰهِيْمُ . قَدْ صَدَّقْتَ...

And when they both submitted and he put him down upon his forehead. And We called to him, 'O Abraham, You have fulfilled the dream (al-ru'ya)...' (37:103-105)

Here, too, everyone has interpreted it as referring to a dream. Imam Ibn Kathir has written, citing Abdullah ibn Abbas (RA):

> *Ibn Abbas (RA) stated that the dreams of the prophets are a form of revelation. Then he recited the verse where Abraham said, "My son, I have seen in a dream that I am sacrificing you, so what do you think?" (Tafsir Ibn Kathir 7/24)*

c. *The Vision of Prophet Yusuf (PBUH) in Surah Yusuf:*

اِذْ قَالَ يُوسُفُ لِاَبِيهِ يَٰٓاَبَتِ اِنِّى رَاَيْتُ اَحَدَ عَشَرَ كَوْكَبًا وَّالشَّمْسَ وَالْقَمَرَ رَاَيْتُهُمْ لِى سَٰجِدِينَ . قَالَ يَٰبُنَىَّ لَا تَقْصُصْ رُءْيَاكَ عَلَىٰٓ اِخْوَتِكَ فَيَكِيدُوا لَكَ كَيْدًا ۗ اِنَّ الشَّيْطٰنَ لِلْاِنْسَانِ عَدُوٌّ مُّبِينٌ.

> *This is the story of when Yusuf said to his father: 'Father, I saw eleven stars the sun, and the moon in my dream; I saw them prostrating to me.' His father replied: 'My son, do not share your dream (al-ru'ya) with your brothers, lest they plot against you, for Satan is indeed a clear enemy to man.' (12:4-5)*

On these verses, Ibn Kathir writes:

> *Ibn Abbas (RA) stated that the dreams of the prophets are a form of revelation. Commentators have said that the eleven stars in this context refer to the eleven brothers of Yusuf (Joseph), peace be upon him. The sun and moon symbolize his father and mother. Upon hearing this dream and understanding its interpretation, Yaqub (Jacob), peace be upon him, emphasized that Yusuf should not repeat it to his brothers, as the interpretation of this dream was that his brothers would bow down to him. (4/317-318)*

d. *The Interpretation of the Vision of Prophet Yusuf (PBUH) in Surah Yusuf:*

فَلَمَّا دَخَلُوا عَلَىٰ يُوسُفَ اٰوَىٰٓ اِلَيْهِ اَبَوَيْهِ وَقَالَ ادْخُلُوا مِصْرَ اِنْ شَآءَ اللّٰهُ اٰمِنِينَ. وَرَفَعَ اَبَوَيْهِ عَلَى الْعَرْشِ وَخَرُّوا لَهُ سُجَّدًا ۚ وَقَالَ يَٰٓاَبَتِ هٰذَا تَأْوِيلُ رُءْيَاىَ مِنْ قَبْلُ قَدْ جَعَلَهَا رَبِّى حَقًّا ...

When they entered Yusuf's presence, he made a place for his parents and said, 'Enter Egypt, God willing, in safety.' He seated his parents upon the throne, and they all prostrated before him. Yusuf proclaimed: 'O my father, this is the fulfillment of my earlier dream (ru'yaya). My Lord has made it reality...' (12: 99-100)

Imam Ibn Kathir writes:

Sulaiman said that there was a forty-year gap between seeing the dream and its interpretation becoming apparent. Abdullah bin Shaddad mentioned that it does not usually take longer than this for a dream's interpretation to occur. This is the maximum duration. (4/353)

e. The Vision of the King of Egypt in Surah Yusuf:

وَقَالَ الْمَلِكُ إِنِّي أَرَىٰ سَبْعَ بَقَرَاتٍ سِمَانٍ يَأْكُلُهُنَّ سَبْعٌ عِجَافٌ وَسَبْعَ سُنْبُلَاتٍ خُضْرٍ وَأُخَرَ يَابِسَاتٍ ۖ يَا أَيُّهَا الْمَلَأُ أَفْتُونِي فِي رُؤْيَايَ إِن كُنتُمْ لِلرُّؤْيَا تَعْبُرُونَ .

The king said, 'I see in my dream seven fat cows being eaten by seven lean cows, and seven green ears of corn and another seven dry. O my chiefs, explain to me my dream (ru'yāya) if you can interpret dreams.' (12: 43)

Imam Ibn Kathir has interpreted this as follows:

This is the dream of the king of Egypt. Divine providence had decreed that Yusuf (Joseph), peace be upon him, would emerge from the prison with honor and respect. To bring this about, God caused the king of Egypt to have a dream that left him astonished. (Tafsir Ibn Kathir 4/335)

It is evident from this detail that the word 'dream' has appeared seven times throughout the Noble Qur'an. Of these instances, four refer to noble prophets, while two are about an ordinary man, the king of Egypt. All the places mentioned above have been enumerated. In all cases, except for once in Surah Al-Isra, both the earlier and later scholars interpret *ru'ya* in its usual sense as a dream. In these instances, they show no hesitation whatsoever. Only in Surah Al-Isra does the term diverge from its common meaning without an explicit rationale. Deviating a word from its normal, established meaning without clear reason opposes the accepted norms of language and elocution. Such action is tantamount to misrepresenting the speaker's intention or putting words into the speaker's mouth, which is indisputably impermissible[42].

Books of Hadith

Let us examine some references from hadiths:

...ان ابا هريرة، قال: سمعت رسول الله صلى الله عليه وسلم، يقول: لم يبق من النبوة إلا المبشرات، قالوا: وما المبشرات؟ قال : الرؤيا الصالحة.

Abu Huraira (RA) narrates that the Messenger of Allah (PBUH) said: 'Prophethood has ended, but glad tidings remain.' People asked: 'What are these glad tidings?' The Prophet (PBUH) said: 'Good dreams.' (Bukhari, No: 6990)

والرؤيا ثلاثة : فرؤيا الصالحة بشرى من الله، ورؤيا تحزين من الشيطان، ورؤيا مما يحدث المرء نفسه، فإن راى احدكم ما يكره فليقم فليصل ولا يحدث بها الناس.

The Prophet (PBUH) said: 'Dreams are of three types: a good dream that is from Allah, a distressing dream that is from Satan, and a dream that reflects one's own thoughts. So, when any one of you sees a bad dream, let him get up and perform prayer, and not narrate it to people.' (Muslim, No: 6042)

---

[42] This is an unintentionally foolish task, much like what some self-proclaimed interpreters of the Qur'an have done in our time, creating an Arabic lexicon for the extraction of their desired meanings from the divine book, which has no connection to the Arabic language or human speech. For understanding this matter, one can refer to the exegeses of Sir Syed Ahmad Khan and Ghulam Ahmad Parvez, where explanations of words and terms such as Paradise, Angels, Resurrection, and Hereafter can be observed as examples.

عن ابى قتادة، عن النبى صلى الله عليه وسلم، قال: الرؤيا الصالحة من الله،
والحلم من الشيطان، فإذا حلم فليتعوذ منه، وليبصق عن شماله، فإنها لا تضره.

*Narrated by Abu Qatada (RA), the Prophet (PBUH) said:
'Good dreams are from Allah, and bad dreams are from Satan.
So, if anyone sees a bad dream, he should seek refuge with Allah
from its evil and spit to his left side. Then it will not harm him.'
(Bukhari, No: 6986)*

عن عائشة ام المؤمنين، انها، قالت: اول ما بدئ به رسول الله صلى الله
عليه وسلم من الوحى الرؤيا الصالحة فى النوم، فكان لا يرى رؤيا إلا جاءت
مثل فلق الصبح.

*Narrated by Ummul Mu'minin Aisha (RA): 'The series of
revelations to the Prophet Muhammad (PBUH) commenced
with good dreams. Whatever he saw in his dreams would come
to him in the morning as clear as daylight.' (Bukhari, No: 3)*

Similarly, this term *ru'ya* recurs numerous times in various hadiths,
where it typically refers to the experience of dreaming while asleep. An
important instance is when hadith scholars select titles for dream-
related traditions in their collections, opting to use the same term to
denote the subject matter. Here are some examples from Sahih
Bukhari:

- *Bāb Ru'ya Yusuf* (The chapter on the dream of Joseph)

- *Bāb Ru'ya Ibrāhīm Alayhis-Salām* (The chapter on the
  dream of Abraham, peace be upon him)

- *Bāb Ru'ya al-Layl* (The chapter on dreams at night)

- *Bāb al-Ru'ya bi-n-Nahār* (The chapter on dreams during the
  day)

- *Bāb Ru'ya an-Nisa* (The chapter on the dreams of women)

- *Bāb Mā Budi'a bihi Rasūlullāh Sallallahu Alayhi wa
  Sallam min al-Waḥy al-Ru'ya al-Saliḥah* (The chapter on

how the Messenger of Allah (PBUH) began to receive revelation through true dreams)

- *Bāb al-Ru'ya min Allah* (The chapter on good dreams being from Allah)

- *Bāb al-Ru'ya al-Saliḥah Juz' min Sittatin wa-Arba'īna juz'an min al-Nubuwwah* (The chapter on a good dream being one part of forty-six parts of Prophethood)

- *Bāb al-Tawāṭu' 'alā al-Ru'ya* (The chapter on the concurrence of dreams, meaning when several people see the same dream)

- *Bāb Ru'ya Ahl al-Sujūn wa al-Fasād wa al-Shirk* (The chapter on the dreams of prisoners and the people of corruption and polytheism) [43].

Arabic vocabulary and the contents mentioned in the Qur'an and hadith make it evident as daylight that the word *ru'ya* commonly means a dream. While it is true that in some lexicons, secondary or additional meanings such as *ru'yatu 'ayn* (seeing with the eyes) or metaphorical interpretations of witnessing something in wakefulness are mentioned, and the word is used in Arabic discourse in figurative, metaphorical, and allusive styles as per customary usage, this does not mean that the word, in its literal usage, carries any meaning other than that of a dream.

It is a basic rule of language and communication that words take on their most recognized meanings. To utilize them in an unfamiliar sense or to infer that they hold unusual or alien meanings contradicts the essence of language. The reason lies in the fact that the primary function of language is to facilitate communication, which can only be effective through words and definitions that are known and understood by the audience. Uncommon and seldom used terms do not serve in conveying the intent of the speaker, nor are they interpreted clearly by the listener. This principle is universal across all

---

[43] The titles can be found in the index of Sahih Bukhari, in the Book of Interpretation of Dreams.

languages and modes of discourse[44]. When it comes to comprehending the Holy Qur'an, this guideline is considered a crucial foundation. The Qur'an asserts that it is revealed in *Bi-lisānin 'arabiyyin mubīn*, meaning in a clear and plain Arabic tongue, and it is *Ghayra dhī 'iwaj* – devoid of ambiguity, confusion, and deficiency[45].

Although the foundational lexicons do encompass linguistic, symbolic, specialized, and obscure meanings alongside the conventional and commonly used ones, this does not suggest a discordance of understandings. The objective is to enclose an exhaustive array and to gather the meanings extensively. The compiler desires that the readers are informed about the multifaceted and varied usages of the word. Consequently, isolating a preferred meaning listed under a word in a lexicon and deducing that it conveys only that specific sense within a particular context of speech is against the accepted rules of syntax and language use.

<hr />

2. Reality of Citing Al-Mutanabbi's Verse as Evidence

In reference to considering the word *ru'ya* as signifying seeing something while awake, evidence is derived from a verse by Abu Tayyib al-Mutanabbi[46]. Ibn Hajar al-Asqalani has based his argument on this verse in his explanation of the verse of *Isra* in the book *Fath al-Bari*:

> *And those who have used 'al-ru'ya' in the sense of wakefulness, among them is a poet. His saying goes: 'Wa ru'yak ahla fi al-'uyun min al-ghamad.' (Your vision is sweeter to the eyes than*

---

[44] The only exceptions are the statements which lack grammatical and linguistic depth or those in which the speaker intends to create ambiguity and confusion instead of clarifying his point to the audience.

[45] Surah Al-Shuara 26:192-195; Surah Al-Zumar 39:28

[46] Abu al-Tayyib Ahmad ibn al-Husayn al-Kufi, known as Al-Mutanabbi. He was born in 303 AH and died in 354 AH. He was a renowned Arab poet who had a significant influence on Arabic literature. He also claimed prophethood.

sleep). (5/673)

The argument about this verse revolves around the fact that here, the word *ru'ya* is not associated with a dream. That is, it is not about an imaginary scene witnessed during sleep but rather refers to perception while being fully conscious. In our view, Ibn Hajar's assertion that the term *ru'ya* in this context does not mean a dream and hence should imply seeing with open eyes is unequivocally accurate[47]. However, the question remains: does this argument lead to the conclusion drawn by Ibn Hajar and other scholars, that the word *ru'ya* is used both for seeing in sleep and for seeing in wakefulness, and that in Surah Al-Isra it is used in the latter sense? We consider the response to this query to be negative.

To unravel this, it is essential to evaluate the following three aspects:

1. Does the word, phrase, or structure of the verse in question necessitate looking beyond the Book of God to determine the intent of the speaker?

2. Is Abu Tayyib al-Mutanabbi counted among those poets whose poetry is deemed admissible for interpreting the Qur'an?

3. Is there any congruity or resemblance between the scheme or mode of articulation of the poem and that of the verse?

Addressing these three queries is vital for grasping the matter

---

[47] The word *ru'ya* in this poem is used to convey the meaning of "seeing with awake eyes." Its interpretation can be understood in the following way: In the poem, the word *ru'ya* is juxtaposed with *ghamad* (sleep). It is used in a non-literal sense. However, it is acknowledged that dreams and sleep are inherently connected; they cannot be mutually exclusive. Therefore, although it is mentioned in relation to the eyes, the reality is that seeing a dream has no connection with the eyes; it is related to the heart and mind. In this context, it is not feasible to interpret *ru'ya* as a dream seen during sleep. When this is not feasible, it is necessary to determine its meaning in opposition to *ghamad* (sleep) and in line with *al-'uyun* (eyes). In this case, the meaning of *ru'ya* would be *ru'yatu ayn* meaning "seeing with the eyes." Interpreting it as a dream becomes implausible.

thoroughly. Neglecting them while building an argument is not in alignment with the established methodologies for Qur'anic exegesis and linguistic principles. In our assessment, the answer to all three questions is negative, therefore the verse by Al-Mutanabbi cannot be considered valid evidence.

The verse from Surah Al-Isra does not require an interpretation that necessitates the confirmation from Classical Arabic to comprehend the word or style. The need for such a confirmation might arise when the word or style is unfamiliar, ambiguous, susceptible to multiple interpretations, lacks a clear indication of its meaning, or is used in a metaphorical manner. In the preceding discussions, it has been conclusively demonstrated that the word *ru'ya* is not unusual, ambiguous, or conjectural in its denotation[48]. It is a commonly known term in the Arabic lexicon, with a singular meaning of 'dream.' Its usage is always explicit, unambiguously conveying its meaning and relevance. In the Qur'an and hadith, whenever *ru'ya* is mentioned, it conveys this particular and customary meaning. Additionally, in the aforementioned verse, it is employed in its literal sense and not as a metaphor. Consequently, there is no obscurity in the employment of *ru'ya* in the verse that would necessitate external linguistic evidence to grasp its meaning.

Regarding Al-Mutanabbi, it is acknowledged that his poetic works are not applicable for facilitating the understanding of the Qur'an. He is a poet from the Abbasid period and is categorized among the fourth category (out of a total of four categories) of Arabic poets, whereas it is established that for linguistic clarification regarding the Qur'an and Hadith, only works from the foremost two categories of Arab poets are valid. Abdul Qadir bin Umar al-Baghdadi states in the renowned text on Arabic language and literature, *Khizanat al-Adab wa Lubb Lubab Lisan al-Arab*:

> *The texts used as evidence for linguistic matters can be divided into two categories: those in poetic form and those that are not.*

---

[48] The Noble Qur'an was revealed in clear Arabic language, therefore there is no ambiguity in understanding its three levels of meaning.

The first category, poetry, has been classified by scholars into four groups. The first group consists of the pre-Islamic poets (Shu'ara al-Jahiliyyah), such as Imru' al-Qais and Al-A'sha. The second group includes the Mukhadramin, those who lived during both the pre-Islamic and Islamic periods, such as Labid and Hassan ibn Thabit. The third group comprises the early Islamic poets (Mutaqaddimin), also known as Islamiyyin. These are individuals from the early Islamic era, such as Jarir and Al-Farazdaq. The fourth group includes the later poets (Muwalladin), also referred to as Muhdithin. This group includes all poets who came after the first three groups up until our present time, such as Bashar ibn Burd and Abu Nuwas.

There is consensus regarding the first two groups that their poetry can be used as a basis for linguistic evidence.

The existence or resemblance of compositional style between a poem and a Qur'anic verse holds no weight. The reason being that the term *ru'ya* in the verse is utilized in its actual meaning, whilst Al-Mutanabbi has employed it metaphorically. Anyone well-versed in expression and rhetorical art would know that a term's literal and metaphorical applications cannot serve as dependable illustrations for one another. This is because the metaphorical usage renders the word's significance and application vastly different from its literal context. It signifies an alternate application of the word, which stands distinct and separate from its original meaning. Hence, the metaphorical context does not provide a reliable basis for logical reasoning or exemplification when compared to the literal context. This concept can be illustrated with a few instances from Urdu poetry.

Take for example the opening lines of Allama Iqbal's poem Mother's Dream where dream is denoted with literal significance:

Main soyi jo ik shab to dekha yeh khwaab

Barha aur jis se mera iztirāb

Yeh dekha ke main ja rahi hoon kahin

Andhera hai aur raah milti nahin

I slept one night and had this dream (Khwab),
Which escalated my restlessness even more.

I saw that I am going somewhere,
It's dark, and the path is not found.

Now, notice the metaphorical use of 'dream' in another verse from Allama's *Khizr-e-Rah*:

عام حریت کا جو دیکھا تھا خواب اسلام نے

اے مسلماں، آج تو اُس خواب کی تعبیر دیکھ

The dream (khwab) of general freedom Islam saw,
O Muslim, witness today the interpretation of that dream.

Here, the Poet of the East has anthropomorphized the faith of Islam and articulated that it envisioned a 'dream' about human freedom. Evidently, Islam is not an entity that slumbers and experiences dreams. Thus, in this instance, 'dream' is not literal but serves as a metaphor to convey a vision or ideology. Consider the lines by Mir Taqi Mir:

ہوا ہے خواب ملنا اُس سے شب کا

کبھو آتا ہے وہ مہ خواب میں اب

The meeting her at night was a mere dream,
Now she sometimes appears in the moonlight of dreams.

Here, Mir employs 'dream' in two contexts – metaphorically to imply 'unattainable' and then literally meaning 'experienced during sleep'.

From these examples, any individual fluent in a language can discern the difference between a term's literal and metaphorical usage, and why the latter cannot be used for explanation or as evidence when discussing the former. This principle holds for any word in any language that possesses both literal and metaphorical connotations.

After this explanation, let us now try to understand how the word *ru'ya* in the verse of Abu Tayyib al-Mutanabbi is used in a metaphorical sense. For this purpose, it would be appropriate to consider the verse in its context:

إذا اعتل سيف الدولة اعتلت الأرض

ومن فوقها والناس والكرم المحض

When Saif al-Dawlah falls ill, it is as if the earth itself becomes unwell, and everything upon it is overcome with grief and sorrow — including both the people and the pure benevolence and generosity (which also seem to fall ill).

وكيف انتفاعى بالرقاد وإنما

بعلته يعتل فى الأعين الغمض

How can I find solace in sleep when his (Saif Al-Dawlah's) illness has even sickened sleep in the eyes? (Hence sleep did not come, and I stayed awake all night gazing at you, Saif Al-Dawlah).

مضى الليل والفضل الذى لك لا يمضى

ورؤياك أحلى فى العيون من الغمض

Now the night has passed, but the generosity of your (presence) continues (if I had slept tonight, surely the dreams of your visage would have sweetened my sleep), but this waking dream (in which I see you with open eyes), is far sweeter to my eyes than sleep (those dreams).

When you read the verse, it itself tells us that here *ru'ya* is used in a metaphorical meaning. In sleep, a person sees sweet dreams (*ru'ya*) that make the sleep delightful. From this common experience, the poet alludes to and says about his patron that instead of dreaming sweet dreams in sleep, I have stayed awake gazing at you, and this waking dream (sweet vision) is sweeter than the dreams (*ru'ya*) in sleep. This is the meaning of the verse, and it is supported by the previous verses as well.

The metaphorical use of words is a common practice in language and expression. Every language is adorned with it. We elevate the word from its literal meaning and, based on some commonality, adopt the method of simile, metaphor, or allusion, and use it in a completely different meaning. When we say to our nation that Pakistan is the dream of the Poet of the East, or when we tell our son that I have dreamed a lot for you, it doesn't mean the dreams we have while asleep. For further understanding, let's look at some Urdu verses that use the word dream. You will realize how varied and diverse the metaphorical use of the word can be:

Allama Iqbal says:

یہ حکم تھا کہ گلشن کن کی بہار دیکھ

ایک آنکھ لے کے خوابِ پریشاں ہزار دیکھ

This was the command: to behold the spring of 'Gulshan Kon.'
With one eye, perceive a thousand troubled dreams.

Here, Iqbal has used the word 'dream' to mean 'seeing with the eye'. This technique of allusion is roughly the same as the one Al-Mutanabbi used in his verse. It means that nature has provided the human eyes to see terrifying dreams, as the poet here adopts the depiction of seeing dreams with eyes.

In another verse by Iqbal, youth has been metaphorically referred to as a dream:

لکھی جائیں گی کتاب دل کی تفسیریں بہت

ہوں گی اے خواب جوانی، تیری تعبیریں بہت

78

Many interpretations of the heart's book will be written,
Oh dream of youth, you will have many interpretations.

Here is Mirza Ghalib's famous verse:

ہے غیبِ غیب جس کو سمجھتے ہیں ہم شہود

ہیں خواب میں ہنوز، جو جاگے ہیں خواب میں

What we think of as presence is still mysterious and unseen,
Those who are awake in dreams are still in a dream while awake.

Here, Ghalib has illustrated the unique situations of waking up in a dream and dreaming within a dream.

In the following verse of Mir, the word 'dream' has been used metaphorically to mean sleep:

گزری ہے شب خیال میں خوباں کے جاگتے

آنکھیں لگا کے اُس سے میں ترسوں ہوں خواب کو

I have spent the night awake, lost in thoughts of the beloveds,
Fixing my gaze upon them, I now yearn for dreams to come.

See an interesting usage of the word in the following two verses of Mir where the word 'dream' is literally in its actual sense, but figuratively it is used for metaphorical meaning:

سن کان کھول کر کہ تنک جلد آنکھ کھول

غافل یہ زندگانی فسانہ ہے، خواب ہے

جو کچھ نظر پڑے ہے، حقیقت میں کچھ نہیں

عالم میں خوب دیکھو تو عالم ہے خواب کا

Listen carefully, open your ears swiftly those eyes,
Careless one, this life is but a tale, a dream.

Whatever seems apparent, there is nothing in reality,
If you look carefully in the world, the world is nothing more
than a dream.

Respected Dr. Khurshid Rizvi used 'dream' in its actual sense in one
of his verses and clarified its condition with excellent skill:

عالمِ خواب کا عقدہ نہیں کھلتا، یعنی

آنکھ باقی نہ رہے اور تماشا رہ جائے

The knot of the dream world does not unravel, as if,
The eye no longer remains and the spectacle persists.

In another verse, he has considered the tasks of open eyes for vision
and perception to be effective for the world of dreams and ineffective
for the world of awakeness, thus creating a unique meanings of self-
awareness.

مری نگاہ نے خوابوں میں خود کو پہچانا

کہ جاگتے میں جو گزری، وہ بے بصر گزری

My vision recognized itself in dreams,
For what passed while awake was without sight.

Consider a verse from the poem by the Javed Ahmed Ghamidi. Here,
the dream is utilized both literally and metaphorically, artistically
merging the concepts of the dream world and the waking world to
express the inner emotions of the heart:

مرے ندیم، کئی بار آخرِ شب میں

مرے چراغ کی لو میں بنی تری تصویر

کنارِ آب چناروں میں ڈوب کر ابھری

خیالِ خواب میں خوابِ خیال کی تعبیر

My friend, many a time at the conclusion of night,

Beneath the flickering light of my lamp, your figure took shape.

Immersed in the currents beneath the Chinar trees, it appeared
A dream within contemplation, deciphered in the reverie of
thought.

It's a frequent occurrence that upon awakening, dreams dissolve from memory. Hence, matters forgotten are often likened to dreams metaphorically. In the Urdu language, the phrase 'khwab o khayal' (dream and thought) is regularly used. The esteemed teacher has this to say in a verse:

نہ وہ زماں ہے، نہ وہ مکاں ہے، عجیب منظر بدل رہا ہے

ہوا ہے خواب و خیال وہ بھی، جو تھا کبھی دیدہ و شنیدہ

Neither that time remains, nor that place—the scene is
strangely shifting.

Even what was once seen and heard has now become mere
dream and illusion.

These instances serve to demonstrate the entwining of metaphor with reality. Were we to delve deeply, we could endlessly populate pages with discourse. To wrap up, here are two couplets by the contemporary poetess Parveen Shakir in her ghazal, where dream is a metaphor for enchanting visions. This mirrors Al-Mutanabbi's style, where the word *ru'ya* hints at the attractive features of a person she admired:

آنکھوں سے میری، کون مرے خواب لے گیا

چشم صدف سے گوہر نایاب لے گیا

کچھ کھوئی کھوئی آنکھیں بھی موجوں کے ساتھ تھیں

شاید اُنھیں بہا کے کوئی خواب لے گیا

Who has plucked the dream from my eyes?
From the mollusk's stare, a precious pearl was purloined.

There, amidst the waves, were lost-looking eyes,
It seems someone has snatched them away with the dream.

From this explanation, it's abundantly clear that interpreting a word differently from its conventional and known meaning and using it in variant contexts as proof is linguistically unsound. If we were to adopt this practice in text interpretation, based on the above verses, we would be compelled to augment the meanings of 'dream' to encompass 'sight', 'alertness in slumber', 'futility of effort', 'vanishing of entities', 'forgetfulness', amongst numerous other implications.

It would be akin to construing Ghalib's verse,

غالب کو برا کہتے ہو، اچھا مرے آگے

"You call Ghalib bad, but praise him in my presence" - as if it meant to speak ill of Ghalib behind his back yet praise him before the speaker. Or interpreting Iqbal's declaration, 'Life is a surge of milk, chisel, and massive rock' as if the essence of life includes, apart from existence, a stream of milk, a sculptor's tool, and a hefty stone. This would amount to a massacre of language and articulation, achievable only by one who deciphers language through logic rather than conversational use.

Furthermore, it's paramount in our discourse to acknowledge that the text itself dictates whether a word is intended literally or metaphorically. The authority to discern the meaning doesn't belong to the listener, reader, annotator, translator, or interpreter based on personal perspective or opinion. To assume otherwise is tantamount to attributing one's own words to the speaker and distorting their intent, an act devoid of any legitimacy in linguistic articulation.

One might then inquire: how do we deduce a word's implied meaning within a text? The answer is through context, coherence, sentence structure, and the written expression. These elements offer clear signals about the intended message and utilization of the word. These very signals serve as the cornerstone in disputes around interpretations. Using these criteria, we discern the denotations of nouns and verbs in the text, stating, for instance, that 'lion' in one sentence signifies the jungle beast and in another symbolizes courage, that *Aftab* (sun) and *Mahtab* (moon) sometimes denote celestial bodies, and other times beloved or exalted individuals, and that 'dream' can mean a vision in one context, ideation in another, or sleep in yet another. Much like verbs, where 'sleeping' and 'awakening' might not merely indicate the physical states but could also metaphorically imply negligence and proactiveness.

The excerpt from *Meezan* could be helpful in understanding aspects of language and expression:

> *The words and styles of every living language in the world, which indicate certain meanings, are all based on continuous use and are absolutely definite in every respect. Dictionaries, grammar, and other such sciences describe this continuity. When considering these elements, the truthfulness or falsehood of those transmitting the language, and their number, is not a topic of discussion. Words and expressions that are considered rare or uncommon are described as such not because of their intrinsic meaning, but due to their infrequent or abundant usage, and in light of the knowledge and awareness of the audience. The usage of a word and the evolution of its meaning are inseparable; as long as a word is in use, its meaning accompanies it. We might be ignorant of a word's meaning and we can err in its interpretation, but it is inconceivable that it has ever been used without a defined meaning or that it has been utilized arbitrarily in any era. The understanding of devices such as metaphor, euphemism, generality, and specificity continues concurrently as well. In all world languages, this is a shared legacy of human culture. Consider the sentences 'The lion is the king of the jungle' and 'Which lion's arrival makes the desert shiver—an individual might mistake metaphor for reality, but this collective human consciousness is unwavering. It is this collective understanding that corrects an individual's mistakes. This is the fundamental truth about language that enables us to communicate with assurance, confident that others will comprehend our intended message. Consider the documents that are written every day, the*

verdicts handed down, directives issued, information shared, and knowledge conveyed—if even for a moment we doubt that the relationship between words and their meanings is definite, then everything would become entirely nonsensical. (32-33)

3. Reality of Citing Al- Ra'i's Verse as Evidence

The word *ru'ya* is presented as evidence in the sense of physical sight in a couplet by the Umayyad-era poet, Ra'i[49]:

فكبر للرؤيا وهش فؤاده

It was upon such a ru'ya that he exclaimed 'Allahu Akbar' and his heart became joyful.

It is said that a linguistic poet used *ru'ya* not to mean seeing in a dream but seeing with open eyes. This indicates that in the Arabic language, the term also conveys the sense of physical sight. Thus, interpreting it as physical sight in verse 60 of Surah Al-Isra aligns with language and expression. The meaning is that if this is interpreted as an observation made in a state of wakefulness, rather than a non-physical or unreal vision of a dream, it would align with the established usages of the word.

In this context, the following reference from "Lisan al-Arab" is typically mentioned:

قال ابن برى: وقد جاء الرؤيا فى اليقظة،قال الراعى: فكبر للرؤيا وهش فؤاده. وبشر نفسًا كان قبل يلومها. وعليه فسر قوله تعالى: وَمَا جَعَلْنَا الرُّءْيَا الَّتِي اَرَيْنٰكَ اِلَّا فِتْنَةً لِّلنَّاسِ.

Ibn Bari states that the term 'al-ru'ya' can also refer to wakefulness. Al-Ra'i says: 'He magnified the vision, and his

---

[49] Ubaid bin Husayn al-Nimiri bin Muawiyah bin Jundal Al-Ra'i is a renowned poet from the Basra region. He is counted among the poets of the Umayyad era. Jarir and Farazdaq are among his contemporaries. He died in 90 AH corresponding to 709 AD.

heart rejoiced. And he gave glad tidings to a soul that had previously blamed itself.' Based on this, the interpretation of Allah's statement is given: 'And We did not make the vision which We showed you except as a trial for the people.' (8/297)

This argument is, in our view, another example of the same error that happened with the poetry of Mutanabbi. Namely, first, the metaphorical sense of *ru'ya* was mistakenly superimposed on its actual meaning, then this misinterpretation was used to justify new usages of the word. This was followed by applying this new meaning as literal in the verse. The matter has become slightly convoluted. Let's clarify it with an example:

Consider these verses from Urdu poets where *dil* (heart) is metaphorically used to mean home or as its equivalent:

دل میں ذوقِ وصل و یادِ یار تک باقی نہیں

آگ اِس گھر میں لگی ایسی کہ جو تھا جل گیا

In the heart, there's no longer longing for union or remembrance of the beloved,

The fire that was kindled in this house has consumed all that existed. (Ghalib)

دل کے تئیں آتش ہجراں سے بچایا نہ گیا

گھر جلا سامنے پر ہم سے بجھایا نہ گیا

The heart could not be saved from the flames of separation,

The house blazed before our eyes, beyond our power to douse. (Mir)

ترا کیا کام اب دل میں غم جانانہ آتا ہے

نکل اے صبر اِس گھر سے کہ صاحب خانہ آتا ہے

What need have you now to dwell in the heart? Sorrow of the beloved approaches,

Depart, o patience, for the owner from this house returns.
(Ameer)

درد کو پھر ہے مرے دل کی تلاش

خانہ برباد کو گھر یاد آیا

Agony again seeks out my heart,

The ruined dwelling has hearkened to its homestead. (Fani)

جنھیں میں ڈھونڈتا تھا آسمانوں میں زمینوں میں

وہ نکلے میرے ظلمت خانۂ دل کے مکینوں میں

Those whom I sought in the skies and the earth,

Have now emerged from the dusky chambers of my heart.
(Iqbal)

Based on these verses, would it be wise to say that the word 'heart' has been used in the sense of 'house' in them, then the lexicon of this word should also include the definitions of house, abode, or dwelling along with the physical organ and emotions and feelings, so that readers can choose the meaning they find closer to their taste and understanding in the context of the text they are considering? So, for example, if they were to read this verse by Maulana Zafar Ali Khan:

میں اُس کو کعبہ و بت خانہ میں کیوں ڈھونڈنے نکلوں

مرے ٹوٹے ہوئے دل ہی کے اندر ہے قیام اُس کا

I don't need to search for Him in the Kaaba or the idol house;

For He resides within my shattered heart's space.

Would they explain it as – I don't need to seek Allah Almighty in the Kaaba or in the idol house, because He resides in my own broken 'home' – then it would be considered absolutely correct according to language and expression.

In this example, to take 'the broken heart' as 'a broken house' is

86

evidently wrong, which readers can understand with due reflection. For further understanding, one could look back at the previous pages discussing the concept of literal and metaphorical implications.

After this clarification, one should also become acquainted with the metaphorical meaning of the word *ru'ya* used in the mentioned line of 'Ubaid Ibn Hussein an-Nameri al-Ra'i'. When the verse is read in its context, the meaning will become fully clear. The poet says:

ومستنبح تهوى مساقط رأسه

على الرحل فى طخياء طمس نجومها

When the stars of the dark night began to fade, a strange traveler arrived whose head (due to sleepiness and exhaustion from traveling all night) kept falling on the saddle.

رفعت له مشبوبة عصفت لها

صبا تزدهيها مرة وتقيمها

I had kindled a fire for him. A breeze blew over it, which occasionally stirred it and made it stand.

فكبر للرؤيا وهش فؤاده

وبشر نفسًا كان قبل يلومها

(The weary and disheartened) traveler exclaimed 'Allahu Akbar' when he saw this beautiful dreamlike scene and his heart was filled with joy. Then he gave glad tidings to his soul, which he was blaming just a while before.

It's crystal clear that here the poet has used the word *ru'ya* in lieu of *ruyatan* to signify a vision of alluring scenes. The intent is to highlight the unexpected joy the traveler feels amidst the severity of his situation[50]. For the traveler—having just emerged from the trials and

---

[50] In such situations, we also find ourselves saying something like, "It feels like I am dreaming." When we say this, we know that it is not a dream but

tribulations of traveling throughout the night in the desert—the sudden sight of a fire was no less than a delightful dream. The poet chose this style to accentuate this unexpected and extraordinary scenario. On such an occasion, if *ru'ya* had been replaced with the literal sense of *ruyatan*, the desired expression of the theme would not be possible at all. Allama Shahab Khafaji in his book *Sharh Durratul-Ghawas fi Awahamil-Khawas* clarifies, referencing Ibn Barri, that 'Al-Ra'i' used the word *ru'ya* in its metaphorical sense in the stated verse. He writes:

وقال ابن برى الرؤيا وإن كانت فى المنام فالعرب استعملتها فى اليقظة

كثيرًا، فهو مجاز مشهور كقول الراعى...

Ibn Bari states that although ru'ya is commonly used to mean a dream, the Arabs frequently use it to refer to seeing something while awake as well. However, this usage is well-known as a metaphor rather than a literal reality. For example, as Al-Ra'i says...(318)

Nonetheless, the use of the word *ru'ya* here is in no way related to its usage in Surah Al-Isra. Both these styles are completely distinct from each other and share no commonality, resemblance, or similarity. The manner of their use and their respective contexts clearly demonstrate that in the Surah, the word is employed in its real sense while in the poetic verse it has been used metaphorically. Therefore, these two uses cannot be presented as examples of one another.

4. Intendend Meaning of the Phrase *Subhāna alladhī*

The word *Subhān* is an expression of glorification and exaltation.

---

reality. Examples of the metaphorical use of dreams in poetry have been discussed in previous pages.

When used for Allah Almighty, its purpose is to dispel any misconceptions or misunderstandings about His essence and to highlight His attributes. In this context, it signifies that Allah's essence is free from every imperfection or flaw and is characterized by the specific attribute concerning which doubt or misgiving has been raised. This meaning is employed in multiple instances throughout the Noble Qur'an.

So, if Allah's unity is questioned, it would be stated: *Subhāna alladhī wa ta'ala 'amma yushrikoon* (Allah is pure and exalted above what they associate with Him[51]).

If any weakness or inferiority has been attributed to Him, it is said: *Subhāna rabbika rabbil-Izzati Ammā Yasifūn* (Your Lord, the Lord of honor, is far above what they describe[52]).

If His planning and management of affairs have been questioned, then these supplicatory words have been uttered: *Rabbana mā khalaqta hādhā bātilan, subhānaka faqinā adhāba an-nār* (Our Lord, You have not created all this without purpose. You are free from any imperfection of creating anything without a purpose[53]).

If there has been any doubt about His knowledge and wisdom, then the saying of the people of truth has been narrated: *Subhānaka lā ilma lanā illā mā allamtanā, innaka anta al-Alīmu al-Hakīm* (Your being is free from all flaws; we only know as much as You have told us. Indeed, You are the All-Knowing, the Wise[54]).

This is the case with power, lordship, mercy, and His other attributes.

In the verse under discussion, the word *Subhāna* has not come to highlight the attribute of power, as commonly thought, but it has come from the aspect of Allah being All-Hearing and All-Seeing. The verse begins with *Subhāna alladhi asra bi 'abdihi laylan mina al-*

---

[51] Surah Al-Qasas, 28:68

[52] Surah Al-Saffat 37:180

[53] Surah Aale Imran 3:191

[54] Surah Al-Baqarah 2:32

masjidi al-harāmi ilā al-masjidi al-aqsā (Glory be to Him who took His servant by night from the Sacred Mosque to the farthest mosque) and ends with the words *Innahu huwa al-Samī'u al-Basīr* (Indeed, He is the All-Hearing, the All-Seeing). This means that the aspect from which *Subhāna* has appeared shall be determined by the words *al-Samī'u al-Basīr*, and it will be implied that Allah is free from any suspicion that may arise regarding His attributes of being All-Hearing and All-Seeing.

Accordingly, the subject matter of the verse is how the Creator, who endowed the Israelites with the position to bear witness to the religion[55] and entrusted them with the responsibility to exhibit the true faith within their collective existence and testify before the nations of the world in such a manner that the sovereignty of Allah's religion is established in this world[56], could tolerate their persistent shirking of duties and yet allow them to remain in this great position. The fact is, they not only failed to meet the demands of their position but went further and adopted a rebellious and denying attitude towards God. Their disobedience and rebellion eventually escalated to the point where they pursued to murder one of Allah's prophet. Allah, All-Hearing and All-Seeing, was observing their crimes while granting them respite. Now that respite has ended, and He has decided to depose the Israelites from this esteemed position and bestow the responsibility of testimony upon the Prophet who is unlettered and his nation, Ishmaelites[57].

---

[55] In Qur'anic terminology, it means that the truth of the religion is made so clear to other nations that after that, there remains no room for them to deviate from it.

[56] That is, Allah appoints an individual to the position of Messengership or a nation to the position of bearing witness, and through them, He conveys the testimony of the true religion to the level of finality, thereby establishing proof against the addressees. Following this, a minor judgment day is established in the world for the reward and punishment of the addressed people.

[57] This position of bearing witness to the truth was first granted by Allah to

Javed Ahmed Ghamidi writes:

The word Subhān at the beginning of the verse comes from a perspective explained by these attributes. It means that it was the responsibility of God to hold those treacherous people accountable, who, in the words of Jesus, peace be upon him, had turned His house into a den of thieves. After hearing and seeing what the Israelites have been saying and doing in this house, it was inevitable. Hence, God has decided that the trust of this house should be handed over to the unlettered prophet. He was brought here from the Sacred Mosque overnight for this purpose. God is free from all imperfection, so He could not possibly tolerate that a nation, despite such a level of defiance on its part, should be left in charge. It was imperative that He arrange for another in view of the intended objective. He has done this and has entrusted the global responsibility of preaching and testimony to the Ishmaelites. (Al-Bayan 3/63)

From this detailed explanation, it is clear that the word *Subhān* here has not been used to highlight the attribute of divine power but to clarify the attribute of Allah being All-Hearing and All-Seeing. It means that this word serves the purpose of negating or erasing any such suspicion that has or could arise concerning Allah's attribute of being All-Hearing and All-Seeing.

After this explanation, it should also be understood that the journey

---

the branch of Abraham's descendants, the Israelites. When they proved unworthy of it, this responsibility was passed on to the other branch, the descendants of Ishmael. Regarding the consequences and implications of this responsibility, my esteemed teacher wrote in *Meezan* under the title The Mission of the Progeny of Abraham: 'This is the role of the progeny of Abraham. If they adhere to the truth and convey it to all the nations of the world in its pure and unaltered form with full certainty, then in the case of rejection, Allah grants them dominance over these nations. However, if they deviate from this mission, they are subjected to humiliation and subjugation through these very nations. Both the Israelites and the Ishmaelites are currently experiencing this punishment.'

mentioned in *asra bi abdihi laylan mina al-masjidi al-harāmi ilā al-masjidi al-aqsa* — meaning the journey of the Prophet Muhammad (PBUH) from the Sacred Mosque to the Farthest Mosque — was not intended to present a miraculous phenomenon to the Quraysh or to prove the truth of his prophethood through it. The context of the verse, its style of expression, and its underlying message all clarify this point. Allah the Almighty has described this journey as a favor upon the Prophet (PBUH) and has clearly indicated its purpose: *linuriyahu min āyātinā* — 'so that We might show him some of Our signs.' Imam Amin Ahsan Islahi explains in his commentary:

> ... It is said that this journey was made to show His servant some of the signs. What these signs were is not mentioned here. However, the context provides evidence that these imply the traces and observations, and the lights and blessings, with which both of these houses [the Sacred Mosque and the Farthest Mosque] were endowed. It seems clear that the purpose of showing these signs was to make evident to the Prophet (PBUH) Allah's intent that now this trust would be taken away from those unworthy and treacherous and placed in his care. In other words, during this extremely challenging period of his mission, this journey of the Ascension was further confirmation of the glad tidings of Allah's support and victory, and what was to happen was also shown to him. (*Tadabbur-e-Qur'an 4/475*)

It becomes clear that this event was a great glad tiding for the Prophet (PBUH) and a herald of the Lord's selection and favor for the people of faith. It was not directly related to the disbelievers of Quraysh. It was their misfortune that, due to their obstinacy and enmity, they turned this into a trial for themselves. If this argument is clear, then scholars' reasoning around *Subhān* and the entire discussion on physical and spiritual vision becomes irrelevant to the verse of *Isra*.

Here we conclude our discussion. However, there are two additional points to note below. The aim of discussing these points is that if someone insists on the association of the word *Subhān* with God's attribute of power, it should become clear to them that there is no room for such interpretation in the examples of the Qur'an, nor does the narration of the event accept it.

The first point is that even if *Subhān* relates to the attribute of God's power, it is not necessary to tie it to an event or matter that is supernatural or peculiar and alien. From this perspective, it also appears to direct attention to the truths of God's power. The following verses indicate the same:

$$\text{سُبْحٰنَ الَّذِىْ خَلَقَ الْاَزْوَاجَ كُلَّهَا مِمَّا تُنْبِتُ الْاَرْضُ وَمِنْ اَنْفُسِهِمْ وَمِمَّا لَا يَعْلَمُوْنَ.}$$

Glorious is the Being Who made all the pairs of things which the earth sprouts and from among these people themselves too and also of things which they do not know. (36:36)

$$\text{...وَتَقُوْلُوْا سُبْحٰنَ الَّذِىْ سَخَّرَ لَنَا هٰذَا وَمَا كُنَّا لَهُ مُقْرِنِيْنَ.}$$

and say: "Exalted is the being who has put them to our service. We were not capable of bringing them into our control. (43:13)

The second point to consider is that even if the term *Subhān*, which signifies glorification, necessarily indicated something extraordinary or miraculous, it would still not require physical travel as a prerequisite. The reason being, the miraculous nature of physical travel would have only been evident if people had witnessed the ascension and descent of the Prophet Muhammad (PBUH) in their own eyes, which was not the case. Rather, the Prophet (PBUH) simply relayed the events of his journey afterward. Regardless of whether the journey was physical or spiritual, it was effectively a report from the Prophet Muhammad (PBUH). It was akin to his daily expressions of eloquence, where he would inform people of the unseen and unknown matters of the past, present, and future. Thus, for his audience, the primary concern was not the physical or spiritual nature of the journey. Due to the absence of direct observation, both scenarios were equivalent to them. Their true challenge related to the claim presented by the Holy Qur'an and the narrative that the Prophet Muhammad (PBUH) shared the following morning. Their concern was not about the content of the message, but rather the trustworthiness of the messenger. That is why their questions revolved not around the soul or body, but rather around the features and specifics of the mosque. Even when detailed descriptions were provided, they did not inquire whether the Prophet (PBUH) ascended alone, used a mount, or whether the event occurred in a spiritual or physical state. Considering they attributed even more miraculous acts to their idols, sorcerers, and the jinn with whom they interacted, the idea of such an event was not utterly implausible to them.

∿∿∿∿∿∿∿∿

5. Reality of the Argument Based on *Asra bi 'abdihi*

The phrase *Asra bi-fulan* translates to taking someone away during the night. The term *abd* refers to a servant. Hence, *alladhī asra bi 'abdihi* signifies 'The One who took His servant away during the night.' Scholars argue that *asra*, which means to take away, necessitates it being linked with a tangible form or a physical entity. Associating this solely with the soul or the self is deemed incorrect. Additionally, *abd*, which means servant, denotes an entity comprising both soul and body, and its use cannot be restricted to just the soul or the body alone. Dreams encompass conditions relating only to the soul, with the body and its parts not participating, so the act of *asra* and the term *abd* do not fit dream experiences.

On the surface, this argument might seem compelling, yet it lacks foundation in knowledge, reasoning, or linguistic principles. Is a new language crafted or a separate lexicon developed specifically for recounting dreams? It would be hard to identify a greater act of neglect towards language and expression than this viewpoint.

It is a fundamental rule in all languages that the expressions used to describe actions in a state of wakefulness are equally applied to dreams and imagination. One only has to attempt retelling their dream in any language to recognize that the articulation of dream states does not differ from that of wakeful experiences. The only requirement might be to initially specify or clarify that the narrative pertains to a dream.

In the Holy Qur'an, the dreams of Prophet Muhammad (PBUH) and Prophet Abraham (PBUH) are documented in Surah Al-Fath and Surah As-Saffat, respectively. Prophet Muhammad (PBUH) envisioned himself and his companions entering Masjid al-Haram, shaving their heads, and trimming their hair. Prophet Abraham (PBUH) saw himself sacrificing his son Ishmael (PBUH). Both dreams were validated and revealed through Allah's Messengers. The nouns and verbs utilized in their description are identical to those used for conscious events. The pertinent verses are as follows:

لَقَدْ صَدَقَ اللّٰهُ رَسُوْلَهُ الرُّءْيَا بِالْحَقِّ لَتَدْخُلُنَّ الْمَسْجِدَ الْحَرَامَ اِنْ شَآءَ اللّٰهُ اٰمِنِيْنَ مُحَلِّقِيْنَ رُءُوْسَكُمْ وَمُقَصِّرِيْنَ لَا تَخَافُوْنَ فَعَلِمَ مَا لَمْ تَعْلَمُوْا فَجَعَلَ مِنْ دُوْنِ ذٰلِكَ فَتْحًا قَرِيْبًا.

[So, rest assured O Believers!] it is a fact that God had shown His messenger an absolutely true dream. Indeed, if God wills, you will definitely enter the Sacred Mosque with complete peace in a way that you will shave your heads and have hair-cuts; [you will have no fear. It was only that God knew what you did not; so, before this, He blessed you with a victory near at hand. (48:27)

قَالَ يُبُنَيَّ اِنِّيْ اَرٰى فِى الْمَنَامِ اَنِّيْ اَذْبَحُكَ فَانْظُرْ مَاذَا تَرٰى ۚ قَالَ يٰۤاَبَتِ افْعَلْ مَا تُؤْمَرُ سَتَجِدُنِيْ اِنْ شَآءَ اللّٰهُ مِنَ الصّٰبِرِيْنَ.

Abraham said to him [one day]: 'My son! [Since the past few days,] I dream that I am slaughtering you. So reflect; what is your opinion?' He said: 'Father! Do as you are being directed. God willing, you will find me steadfast.' (37:102)

From these verses, it is evident that the Prophet (PBUH) dreamt that Muslims were entering the sacred enclosure of the Kaaba, shaving their heads, and trimming their hair. Similarly, Prophet Abraham (PBUH) dreamt that he was sacrificing his son. The pronouns and verbs expressed in these dreams involve human actions, including those of absence, presence, and addressing, using verbs like 'enter,' 'shave,' 'shorten,' and 'sacrifice,' which apply to beings composed of body and soul. If our scholars were to impose their interpretations here too, they would have to view these occurrences as waking events and interpret the phrases *Laqad Sadaqallahu Rasūlahu al-ru'yā* and *Innī Arā fī al-Manām* as perceptive experiences in a state of wakefulness.

Consider several hadiths where the Messenger of Allah (PBUH) vividly described his dreams through actions:

'I saw two men' - رايت رجلين

'both of them took me away' - اتياني

'Both of them took hold of my hand' - فاخذا بيدى

'Both of them took me to the Holy Land' - فاخرجاني إلى الارض المقدسة

'I am migrating' - انى اهاجر

'I wielded a sword' - انى هززت سيفًا

'I was asleep, and I performing Tawaf' - انا نائم اطوف بالكعبة

These narrations include:

عن سمرة بن جندب، قال: كان النبى صلى الله عليه وسلم إذا صلى صلاةً اقبل علينا بوجهه، فقال: من راى منكم الليلة رؤيا؟ قال: فإن راى احد قصها، فيقول: ما شاء الله، فسالنا يومًا، فقال: هل راى احد منكم رؤيا؟ قلنا: لا، قال: لكنى رايت الليلة رجلين اتيانى، فاخذا بيدى فاخرجانى إلى الارض المقدسة.

Narrated by Samura bin Jundub (RA): The Prophet (PBUH) used to face us after completing the prayer and would ask, 'Who among you had a dream last night?' If anyone had seen a dream, they would narrate it, and he would say whatever Allah willed. One day, he asked, 'Did anyone see a dream last night?' We said, 'No.' He said, 'But I saw last night in which two men came to me, took hold of my hand, and led me to the Holy Land.'

(Sahih Bukhari, No. 1386)

عن ابى موسى، عن النبى صلى الله عليه وسلم، قال. رايت فى المنام انى اهاجر من مكة إلى ارض بها نخل، فذهـب، وهلى إلى انها اليمامة، او هجر، فإذا هى المدينة يثرب.

Narrated by Abu Musa Al-Ash'ari (RA): The Prophet (PBUH) said, 'I saw in a dream that I was migrating from Mecca to a land with palm trees. My mind went to the idea that it might be Yamama or Hajar, but it turned out to be Medina (Yathrib).' (Sahih Muslim, No. 6072)

عن ابى موسى، عن النبى صلى الله عليه وسلم قال: رايت فى رؤياى انى هززت سيفًا فانقطع صدره، فإذا هو ما اصيب من المؤمنين يوم احد.

Narrated by Abu Musa Al-Ash'ari (may Allah be pleased with him): The Prophet (PBUH) said, 'I saw in a dream that I shook a sword and its blade broke. This was manifested in the form of the loss that the Muslims suffered in the Battle of Uhud.' (Sahih Bukhari, No. 4081)

...ان ابا هريرة رضى الله عنه، قال: بينا نحن عند رسول الله صلى الله عليه وسلم إذ قال: بينا انا نائم رايتنى فى الجنة فإذا امراة تتوضا إلى جانب قصر، فقلت: لمن هذا القصر؟ قالوا: لعمر فذكرت غيرته فوليت مدبرًا.

Narrated by Abu Huraira (RA): We were in the company of Allah's Messenger (PBUH) when he said, 'While I was sleeping, I saw myself in Paradise, and there I saw a woman performing ablution beside a palace.' I asked, 'Whose palace is this?' They said, 'It is 'Umar ibn Al-Khattab's.' Then I remembered 'Umar's sense of honor, and so I turned back and left.' (Sahih Bukhari, No. 3242)

عن عبد الله بن عمر، ان رسول الله صلى الله عليه وسلم، قال: بينا انا نائم اطوف بالكعبة.

Narrated by Abdullah bin Umar (RA): The Messenger of Allah (PBUH) said, 'While I was sleeping, I saw myself performing Tawaf around the Kaaba.' (Sahih Bukhari, No. 7128)

حدثنا سمرة، قال: قال رسول الله صلى الله عليه وسلم: اتانى الليلة آتيان فاتينا على رجل طويل لا اكاد ارى راسه طولاً وإنه إبراهيم صلى الله عليه وسلم.

Narrated by Samura (RA): The Messenger of Allah (PBUH) said, 'Two persons came to me last night and took me to a very tall man whose head I could hardly see because of his height, and that man was Abraham (PBUH).' (Sahih Bukhari, No. 3354)

Also, reflect on a dream narrated by Abdullah ibn Umar (RA), which contains nouns and verbs such as *Malikayn Atayani* (two angels approached me), *Fantalaqā bī* (and they took me with them), *Faqāla lī* (and they said to me), paralleling expressions we would use for actual events.

عن ابن عمر، قال: كنت غلامًا شابًا عزبًا فى عهد النبي صلى الله عليه وسلم، وكنت ابيت فى المسجد، وكان من راى منامًا قصه على النبي صلى الله عليه وسلم، فقلت: اللهم إن كان لى عندك خير فارنى منامًا يعبره لى رسول الله صلى الله عليه وسلم، فنمت، فرايت ملكين اتيانى فانطلقا بى فلقيهما ملك آخر، فقال لى: لن تراع، إنك رجل صالح، فانطلقا بى إلى النار فإذا هى مطوية كطى البئر وإذا فيها ناس قد عرفت بعضهم، فاخذا بى ذات اليمين، فلما اصبحت، ذكرت ذلك لحفصة.

Abdullah ibn Umar (RA) narrated: During the time of the Prophet (PBUH), I was a young unmarried man, and I used to sleep in the mosque of the Prophet. It was a common practice that whoever had a dream would narrate it to the Prophet (PBUH). I prayed, 'O Lord, if there is any good in me in this matter, show me a dream that the Prophet (PBUH) can interpret for me.' Then I slept and saw two angels who came to me and took me along with them. Then a third angel joined them. He said to me, 'Do not be afraid; you are a good man.' Then the two angels took

me towards Hell, which was like a well with layers upon layers.
In it were people whom I recognized. Then the two angels took me
towards the right side. (Sahih Bukhari, No. 7030)

6. Argument Based on the Report From Abdullah Ibn Abbas (RA)

Regarding the interpretation of the word *ru'ya* in verse 60 of Surah Al-Isra, the following commentary (*athr*)[58] by Abdullah Ibn Abbas (RA) is often cited:

عن ابن عباس رضى الله عنهما فى قوله تعالى: وَمَا جَعَلْنَا الرُّءْيَا الَّتِيْ اَرَيْنٰكَ إِلَّا
فِتْنَةً لِّلنَّاسِ. قال: هى رؤيا عين اريها رسول الله صلى الله عليه وسلم ليلة اسرى
به إلى بيت المقدس.

Abdullah ibn Abbas (RA) commented on Allah's statement,
'And We did not make the vision which We showed you except
as a trial for the people,' saying that this refers to a ru'ya 'ayn,
meaning a vision seen with the eyes. This was shown to the
Messenger of Allah (PBUH) on the night he was taken to Bayt
al-Maqdis. (Sahih Bukhari, No. 3888)

To properly utilize this commentary as grounds for reasoning, one must first comprehend the significance of his words.

Abdullah Ibn Abbas (RA) stated:

Hiya ru'yā 'ayn arāhā Rasūlullāh laylata usriya bihi ilā Bayt
al-Maqdis (هى رؤيا عين أراها رسول الله صلى الله عليه وسلم ليلة أُسرى
به إلى بيت المقدس.)

In this statement, *ru'yatu 'ayn* (عين رؤية) does not appear. If these words were included, the interpretation involving the visual sight—that is, perception via the eyes—would have been appropriate.

---

[58] This term is used for the narration of the sayings and actions of a Companion (*Sahabi*) or a Follower (*Tābi'i*).

However, this would render the word *arāhā* (اَرَاهَا) redundant and meaningless, as it would imply 'sight that was shown.' The translation would erroneously be: 'This was a visual witnessed by the eyes shown to the Messenger of Allah (PBUH) on the night of *Isra*.'

Here, the term *ru'ya 'ayn* (رؤيا عين) appears. Its literal meaning is 'a vision of the eyes,' that is, 'a dream seen with the eyes.' The accompanying words *arihā* (اريها) are neither redundant nor meaningless; rather, they are indispensable. The reason for this is that the meaning now becomes 'a dream of the eyes was shown,' and the translation is: 'This was a dream seen with the eyes, which was shown to the Messenger of Allah (peace and blessings be upon him) during the night of Isra.'

This makes it clear that Ibn Abbas (RA), neither interpreted this as the *ru'yatan* (seeing) that every sighted person benefits from in a state of wakefulness, nor as the *ru'ya* (dream) that is every person's experience in a state of sleep. Instead, he attributed it to a third category, which is a blend of wakefulness and sleep, and of dream and reality. His point is that just as scenes are observed in dreams, in a similar manner, Allah Almighty presented certain scenes before the eyes of the Prophet (PBUH), which he witnessed while being awake. In essence, according to Ibn Abbas (RA), while it was a dream-like vision, it was shown to the Prophet (PBUH) with open eyes during wakefulness. For explaining this unique nature, he coined the phrase *ru'ya 'aynun urīhā laylatan* (رؤيا عين اريها ليلة). This is a distinctive expression crafted to describe an exceptional situation. It signifies the extraordinary nature of this observation, which is exclusively a characteristic of prophethood, and one that ordinary humans are entirely devoid of. Maulana Abul Kalam Azad, in his commentary *Tarjuman al-Qur'an*, has clarified the statement of Ibn Abbas (RA) from this very perspective. He writes:

> *The conditions and occurrences of the noble Prophets (peace be upon them) relate to such a realm that our common interpretations do not apply. Any interpretation we make will suggest the idea of a state that we commonly experience, but the*

nature of the situations the noble Prophets (peace be upon them) experienced is different. These are matters beyond our senses and common understanding. This is why the impressions of the Companions varied. Those who denied that the events took place in a state of wakefulness leaned towards the belief that the events were not like our physical movement and transportation. Those who insisted that the events occurred in a state of wakefulness argued that these cannot simply be dismissed as dreams. And there is no doubt that both groups were correct in their respective impressions. Even in the Hadith of the Sahihain, it is reported that the Prophet (PBUH) said: I was in such a state that I was neither asleep nor awake, بين النوم واليقظة' (between sleeping and being awake). This clarifies that we cannot categorize this matter as one that occurs in wakefulness, nor as one seen in sleep. It was a state different from both of these, one for which we have no terms or interpretations.

... Abdullah ibn Abbas (RA) was among those Companions who believed that the Mi'raj occurred in a state of wakefulness and was a foremost proponent of this belief. ...And what Hazrat ibn Abbas (RA) referred to by by ru'yā 'ayn urīhā settled the issue, and the reality became clear, to which we have just alluded. That is, whatever happened was indeed a Ru'ya (vision), but what kind of Ru'ya? Was it like what we experience in the realm of dreams? No, it was ru'ya 'ayn. Such a vision in which the eyes are not neglectful; they are alert. What is seen is as if it is being witnessed with the very eyes. (2/430-431)

In summary, there are three kinds of human observation:

1. *Ru'yah*: Observing the external landscape with physical sight while awake.

2. *Ru'ya*: Observing internal manifestations with internal vision while asleep.

3. *Ru'ya 'Ayn*: Observing internal sceneries with physical sight while awake.

With regards to these three types, there are two confirmed differences between Prophets and ordinary people:

1. Firstly, the Prophets experience all three types of observation, whereas ordinary people typically experience only the first two types.

2. Secondly, all three types of the Prophets' observations are true and based on reality[59], unlike those of ordinary people.

According to Abdullah Ibn Abbas (RA), the third type occurred during the incident of Isra[60]. That is, Prophet Muhammad (PBUH) witnessed spiritual scenes with his physical sight while in a state of wakefulness. This interpretation aligns well with the nature of prophetic observations. The reason for this is that such observations of this nature by the Prophet (PBUH) are grounded in reality and are well-documented and acknowledged. A prominent example of this is the incident reported in Sunan an-Nasa'i when, during the eclipse prayer, Paradise was brought before him, and he stepped forward to pluck a cluster of its fruits. The incident has been recorded in Sunan an-Nasa'i in the following words:

عن عبد الله بن عباس، قال: خسفت الشمس فصلى رسول الله صلى الله عليه وسلم والناس معه قالوا: يا رسول الله رايناك تناولت شيئًا فى مقامك هذا ثم رايناك تكعكعت. قال: إنى رايت الجنة او اريت الجنة فتناولت منها عنقودًا ولو اخذته لاكلتم منه ما بقيت الدنيا

---

[59] Therefore, having faith in them is a necessary requirement of belief.

[60] A fourth form, similar to this third form, has emerged in the present era. This is that we watch the circumambulation of the Kaaba, teams playing a match, or people conversing live on the screen of a mobile, computer, or TV. Our watching is also real, and the event is certain, but it cannot be considered the same observation as, for example, us personally performing the circumambulation, being present on the playing field, or participating in the conversation. Therefore, it cannot be called a dream (ru'ya) nor can it be interpreted as ru'ya 'ayn (a dream seen with the eyes). For this different type of view, the term 'live' or 'watching live' has been adopted.

Abdullah Ibn Abbas (RA) narrates that there was a solar eclipse, and the Messenger of Allah (PBUH) along with the people performed the prayer. (After the prayer) the people said to him: O Messenger of Allah, we saw you moving forward as if to take something, and then we saw you stepping back? He replied: 'I saw Paradise, or it was shown to me, and I moved forward to take a bunch of its fruits. Had I taken it, you would have eaten from it for as long as the world remains.' (Sunan an-Nasa'i, No. 1493)

The observation of Paradise in this moment clearly happened while the Prophet (PBUH) was awake. Paradise was presented before the Prophet (PBUH) during the prayer. The narration indicates that it was not just a vision; Paradise appeared vividly, which is why the Prophet (PBUH) reached out to take fruit from it[61].

Similarly, another event took place when the truthfulness of the Prophet's night journey was challenged by the disbelievers. On that occasion, the Al-Aqsa Mosque was also brought before the Prophet (PBUH) in a state of wakefulness[62].

Thus, if the term *ru'ya 'ayn* is employed to describe such an event, there can be no literal objection. This term can be used to express this concept, and similar interpretations are also valid. Imam Shah Waliullah in his book *Hujjat Allah al-Balighah* has used the terms *Ālam al-Mithāl* (world of similitude) and *Barzakh al-'Ālam ash-Shahādah* (barzakh of the realm of testimony) to convey the same meaning. He writes:

The Prophet of God ascended to Masjid Al-Aqsa, then to Sidrat al-Muntaha, and as far as God willed during the Mi'raj, and all this event took place with the body in a state of wakefulness. However, it was in a condition that represented a barrier between the world of similitudes and the world of witnessing,

---

[61] The evidence of this being real and not metaphorical is his reaching out his hand and saying, 'If I had taken a bunch of the fruits of Paradise, you would have eaten from it for as long as the world remains.'

[62] This event has been discussed earlier.

encompassing the rulings of both worlds. The effects of the spirit became dominant over the body, and the states of the spirit took the form of the body. This is why each event within this journey has a distinct interpretation. (2/365)

From this detail, it is clear that the innovative interpretation of Ibn Abbas (RA), *ru'ya 'ayn* (a vision with open eyes), is also understandable, and its application to some incidents mentioned in the hadiths does not contradict the assertion. However, regarding the event of *Isra*, despite appreciating the scholarly greatness of Hazrat Abdullah Ibn Abbas (RA) and recognizing his significance, neither can his interpretation of *ru'ya 'ayn* be accepted, nor can it be considered a waking event. The reason is that God Himself has termed this event as *ru'ya* in the Qur'an. With this clarification in the Qur'an, it is not feasible to interpret it as a physical vision or *ru'ya 'ayn*. If the Qur'an had not elucidated this, then perhaps, based on correlational evidence and analogies, there could have been room for such discourse.

〜〜〜〜〜〜

7. Argument Based from the Phrase *Fitnatan lilnās*

In verse 60 of Surah Al-Isra[63], the phrase *Fitnatan lilnās* (a trial for the people) has been used as a rationale to endorse the physical nature of the journey. The reasoning is that only an incident which is extremely perplexing and whose belief appears implausible can become a source of trial or tribulation. Since witnessing extraordinary events in dreams is a common human occurrence and such occurrences are often dismissed as mere dreamlike imaginings, with their authenticity easily accepted. As a result, they do not become a cause of trial or a test of belief for people. However, if a similar extraordinary event occurs in a state of wakefulness, people become skeptical about its authenticity and are subjected to a test in terms of their acceptance or rejection of it. This is a well-established human experience. Hence, the event of

---

[63] *Wa mā ja'alnā al-ru'yā allatī araynāka illā fitnatan lilnās* (The dream We showed you We made it a trial too for these people)

Isra could only serve as a trial and test for people if it occurred in a state of wakefulness and if the Prophet (PBUH) described it as such. Otherwise, it could neither cause a trial for the people nor could the words *Fitnatan lilnās* apply to it. In our opinion, this argument is flawed, for the foundational reasons outlined below:

Firstly, it presumes that the disbelievers of Quraysh deemed any perplexing event associated with a human or the Prophet Muhammad (PBUH) as impossible. This is not accurate. Due to their myths and beliefs, they were predisposed to believe in all forms of supernatural occurrences linked to their ancestors and deities. Consequently, they had concocted the notion of deeming the Prophet (God forbid) a sorcerer and a magician. Thus, whenever a statement that inspired faith emerged from him or an astonishing event unfolded, they would employ this excuse to dismiss his prophecy. This indicated that they were inclined to anticipate supernatural occurrences from his noble person.

Furthermore, a profound supernatural miracle was occurring before their eyes daily, which was the Divine Speech that was being uttered through the blessed tongue of the Prophet. Its unique and unparalleled mode of articulation was enough for them to concede that the speech could not have been human-made. Even more so, relating it to the Prophet was unfathomable, given that for the first forty years of his life he had never participated in poets' assemblies nor learned the craft of poetry and literature, nor had he created poetry or shown any eloquence. Then, all of a sudden, such words emanated from him that rendered their esteemed poets and literati speechless, forcing them to acknowledge that such speech could not come from a human source. For them, this reality was as astonishing as a celestial ascent.

It becomes evident that the nature of an occurrence being supernatural or astonishing was not a cause for confusion or difficulty for them.

Secondly, when the Prophet (PBUH) informed the gathering the next morning about the details of the structure of Masjid Al-Aqsa—which in itself was an extraordinary miracle, unfolding before the people's very eyes—any doubts they had should have been dispelled at that moment. Yet, this did not happen, and they persisted in denying the event. This also demonstrates that the connection between the event being extraordinary or not and its being a *Fitnatan lilnās* (a trial for the people) is not absolute.

Thirdly, the aforementioned argument leads to the acceptance of the excuse presented by the disbelievers of Quraysh, which neither the words of the verse support nor historical facts validate. This would imply that if Abu Jahl had witnessed the event and seen the Prophet (PBUH) ascending to the heights of the heavens, the event would no longer have been a trial for him. However, the reality is that despite witnessing numerous miracles, he did not believe. In fact, it must be understood that a trial or test arises only from something whose authenticity is certain. Something whose occurrence is uncertain or is beyond comprehension and perception cannot become a trial. In such cases, uncertainty or lack of comprehension becomes an excuse and is considered justifiable both in the eyes of people and before Allah.

Additionally, the solitary experience and testimony of Prophet Muhammad (PBUH), whether in dreams or wakefulness, were simply his narrations to the people, holding equal credibility for them. The transgression of the Quraysh was that they rejected his prophethood out of sheer defiance and obstinacy, even though they considered him reliable and honest in all other respects. Thus, whether the event was a vision or an actual experience, they opted to dismiss it as false. Even had they been eyewitnesses, their denial would persist as Pharaoh rejected Moses's (PBUH) prophecy despite the sorcerers' defeat and their subsequent belief.

Fourthly, Allah has clarified *fitnah* (trial) for the people in the conclusion of verse 60, leaving no room for ambiguity or for pushing any contrived interpretations. The verse explicates:

$$\text{وَنُخَوِّفُهُمْ فَمَا يَزِيدُهُمْ إِلَّا طُغْيَانًا كَبِيرًا.}$$

We are only frightening them of their fate, but this thing is merely increasing them in their extreme rebelliousness.

This means that the cause of the trial (*fitnah*) was not the extraordinary or non-extraordinary nature of the event; rather, it was the warning of the impending outcome. The words *nukhawwifuhum* (We frighten them) serve as conclusive evidence for this. The intended meaning is that this warning and forewarning should have caused them to take heed and work toward self-correction. However, they adopted an attitude of defiance and turned the warning—manifested in the event of *Isra* as a clear indication that their removal from authority had been decreed and that their religion and kingdom were about to be overturned—into a trial and test for themselves. Thus, it is stated in *Al-Bayan*:

> *The issue is not whether a sign is demonstrated to elicit belief. The affliction they suffer from is the malaise of obstinance and defiance. All of this served as a warning and a scare tactic, yet what was the outcome? These three instances only reveal an escalation in their rebellion, just as the Thamud did with the she-camel. (3/95)*

Abu Bakr al-Jassas quotes a statement reflecting similar sentiments from Ibn Abbas (RA):

> *What does this vision imply? The Exalted says: Wa mā Ja'alnā al-ru'yā allatī araynāka illā Fitnatan lilnās (And the vision We showed you was only a trial for the people). According to the narration from Said ibn Jubair on the authority of Ibn Abbas, may Allah be pleased with him, as well as reports from Qatadah, Hasan, Abraham, Mujahid, and Dahhak, this vision is different from the night journey to Jerusalem, that is, Isra. When Prophet Muhammad (PBUH) mentioned it to the polytheists, they denied him. Ibn Abbas (RA) also reported that this vision indicated that the Prophet (PBUH) was shown that he would soon enter Makkah as a victor. (Ahkam Al-Qur'an 5/30)*

At the conclusion of the discussion, it should be understood purely as an academic point that being a trial or tribulation does not necessarily mean that we should take it as something difficult or alien to the comprehension and perception of people. The Qur'an explicitly refutes this idea. Consider verse 20 of Surah Al-Furqan, where the command is stated:

وَمَآ اَرْسَلْنَا قَبْلَكَ مِنَ الْمُرْسَلِيْنَ اِلَّآ اِنَّهُمْ لَيَأْكُلُوْنَ الطَّعَامَ وَيَمْشُوْنَ فِيالْاَسْوَاقِ ۗ وَجَعَلْنَا بَعْضَكُمْ لِبَعْضٍ فِتْنَةً ...

Whichever messengers We sent before you also, all ate food and roamed about in markets. [Believers!] We have made you a trial for one another;...

In the explanation of this verse, Tafsir Ibn Kathir writes:

If Allah Almighty were to grant His prophets abundant worldly wealth and resources, most people would refrain from opposing them out of greed for those benefits. However, since Allah's intent is to test people, He generally keeps His prophets in modest conditions so that they may serve as a trial for others.

It is stated in Sahih Muslim (No. 2865): The Messenger of Allah (peace and blessings be upon him) said that Allah Almighty has declared, 'I will test you, and I will test others through you.'

Maulana Maududi writes in the interpretation of this verse:

That is to say, the disbelievers are a trial for the Messenger and the believers, and conversely, the Messenger and the believers are a trial for the disbelievers. The furnace of oppression and ignorant animosity that the disbelievers had heated up is precisely the means by which it will be proved that the Messenger and his true believers are pure gold. On the other hand, for the disbelievers, the Messenger and the companions of the Messenger are a severe trial. An ordinary person being suddenly proclaimed a Prophet among his community, with no army, wealth, or wondrous attribute other than divine revelation and a pure life, and the inclusion of mostly the poor, slaves, and young people among his early followers, and Allah Almighty leaving those few handfuls of people unprotected among wolves, this is the sieve that prevents the wrong kind of people from approaching the faith and only filters through those who recognize the truth and accept righteousness. (Tafheem al-Qur'an 3/444-445)

Al-Bayan states:

That is to say, your humble state is made a trial for them, and their mocking attitude a trial for you. Because of this, they are denying the truth by saying that if this were the religion of God, then the leaders and nobles of Mecca and Taif would have benefited from it, not these impoverished Muslims. (3/472)

8. Argument Based on People's Reactions

The physical aspects of the journey of *Isra* and *Mi'raj* have also been inferred from the reaction of the people. This inference is based on some narratives in the hadith and history of the Prophetic biography. These describe that the day after the event of *Isra*, when the Prophet (PBUH) informed the people about it, the Quraysh disbelievers denied it, and many Muslims turned apostate. According to scholars, this incident of denial and apostasy is evidence that the journey was incredibly astonishing and seemingly unbelievable. Hence, believing it to be physical is necessary.

The rationale is that if the journey had been merely spiritual, and the Prophet (PBUH) had presented it as something that had happened in a dream, then neither would the disbelievers have rejected it, nor would some Muslims have decided to leave Islam. Everyone would have accepted it as a common human dream. Their denial proves that the event occurred physically while awake. For them, it was intellectually impossible to believe that a journey of two to three months could be completed in one night. In *Tafsir Ibn Kathir*, it is stated:

(The physical nature of the Isra event is evidenced by the use of

the words of tasbih). Declaring the purity and transcendence of Allah necessarily implies that what follows is something immensely grand and significant. However, if this journey is interpreted as a mere dream, it cannot be regarded as a great and extraordinary event (and thus does not align with the use of the words of tasbih). In such a case, neither would the disbelievers of Quraysh have hastened to reject the Prophet (PBUH), nor would a group of those who had embraced Islam have reverted to disbelief. (5/40)

In *Tafsir Al-Qurtubi*, regarding the phrase *Fitnatan lilnās* from verse 60 of Surah Al-Isra, it is written:

Fitnah refers to the apostasy of those who had already accepted Islam. This occurred when the Prophet (peace and blessings be upon him) informed them that he had been taken to (Masjid Al-Aqsa). This event has also been interpreted as a dream seen during sleep. However, this verse refutes the validity of such an interpretation. The reason is that a statement of this nature made in the context of a dream does not become a trial or test (fitnah), nor does anyone deny it upon hearing it. (5/282)

Regardless of the authenticity or inauthenticity of the narratives related to this topic, the aforementioned reasoning and method of reasoning are both unfounded. The underlying assumption, whether consciously or unconsciously held, is that for the audience of Prophet Muhammad (PBUH), the decision to embrace Islam, remain steadfast in it, or to opt for disbelief was heavily influenced by supernatural occurrences and sensory miracles. This notion is rebutted by the Noble Qur'an. In the verses of Surah Al-Isra, Allah the Exalted recounts the demands of the disbelievers of Quraysh for miracles beyond the ordinary and has addressed these demands by instructing the Prophet (PBUH) to tell the Quraysh, 'Am I anything but a man sent as a God's messenger?' Javed Ahmed Ghamidi interprets this to mean:

(To those making such demands, say:) 'When did I claim to be God? When did I ever say that I have power over everything?

When did I declare that the heavens and the earth are in my grasp and that I can do with them as I will? From the very beginning, I have only said this much: that I am a human being, and God has sent me as His Messenger. Tell me, what connection does your making such demands have with what I have said? All these are deeds of God, and I have never made any such claim.' (Al-Bayan 3/109)

The relevant verses are as follow:

وَلَقَدْ صَرَّفْنَا لِلنَّاسِ فِي هٰذَا الْقُرْاٰنِ مِنْ كُلِّ مَثَلٍ فَاَبٰى اَكْثَرُ النَّاسِ اِلَّا كُفُورًا . وَقَالُوا لَنْ نُؤْمِنَ لَكَ حَتّٰى تَفْجُرَ لَنَا مِنَ الْاَرْضِ يَنْبُوعًا . اَوْ تَكُونَ لَكَ جَنَّةٌ مِنْ نَخِيلٍ وَعِنَبٍ فَتُفَجِّرَ الْاَنْهٰرَ خِلٰلَهَا تَفْجِيرًا .

اَوْ تُسْقِطَ السَّمَاءَ كَمَا زَعَمْتَ عَلَيْنَا كِسَفًا اَوْ تَأْتِيَ بِاللّٰهِ وَالْمَلٰئِكَةِ قَبِيلًا . اَوْ يَكُونَ لَكَ بَيْتٌ مِنْ زُخْرُفٍ اَوْ تَرْقٰى فِي السَّمَاءِ وَلَنْ نُؤْمِنَ لِرُقِيِّكَ حَتّٰى تُنَزِّلَ عَلَيْنَا كِتَابًا نَقْرَؤُهُ قُلْ سُبْحَانَ رَبِّي هَلْ كُنْتُ اِلَّا بَشَرًا رَسُولًا .

وَمَا مَنَعَ النَّاسَ اَنْ يُؤْمِنُوا اِذْ جَاءَهُمُ الْهُدٰى اِلَّا اَنْ قَالُوا اَبَعَثَ اللّٰهُ بَشَرًا رَسُولًا . قُلْ لَوْ كَانَ فِي الْاَرْضِ مَلٰئِكَةٌ يَمْشُونَ مُطْمَئِنِّينَ لَنَزَّلْنَا عَلَيْهِمْ مِنَ السَّمَاءِ مَلَكًا رَسُولًا . قُلْ كَفٰى بِاللّٰهِ شَهِيدًا بَيْنِي وَبَيْنَكُمْ اِنَّهُ كَانَ بِعِبَادِهِ خَبِيرًا بَصِيرًا .

We have mentioned in this Qur'an various words of wisdom for people in different ways. Even then most people are adamant on denying. They have said: 'We shall not believe in you unless you make a spring gush from the earth or an orchard of dates or grapes is produced for you; then unless you make many canals run through it. Or unless, as you say, you make the sky fall upon us in pieces or unless you bring God and His angels to stand before us, or you not have a house of gold or you not climb to the sky [right before our eyes]. And We shall not even believe in your climbing unless you reveal a book to us [from there] that we can read' – Tell them: Exalted is my Lord. Am I someone else besides a human being whom the Almighty has sent as a messenger?

When guidance came to them, the only thing that stopped these people from accepting faith was that they said: 'Has God sent a human being as a messenger?' Tell them: Had there been angels on the earth walking about calmly, We would have sent down from the heavens an angel as a messenger to them.

Say: Sufficient is God between you and me as a witness. Undoubtedly, He knows His servants; He is watching them. (17:89-96)

The relevant verses clearly convey that the disbelievers of Quraysh demanded the following types of miracles from the Prophet (PBUH):

1. To cause a spring to gush forth from the earth all of a sudden.

2. To conjure a lush garden of date palms and grapevines, with rivers running through it, out of thin air.

3. To break the sky apart and make it collapse upon us, as they alleged.

4. For Allah and His angels to descend and show themselves to them.

5. To erect a castle of gold for himself.

6. To ascend to the sky and return with a scripture.

Allah could have undoubtedly realized these demands as they were posed and could have shown them through His messenger (PBUH). But rather, He directed His prophet to inform them that he is simply a human who lacks the capabilities to perform such marvels. Imam Amin Ahsan Islahi comments:

In answer to all such demands was the command: Qul subhāna rabbī hal kuntu illā basharan rasūlā, 'Say, My Lord is glorified and free from imperfection; am I anything but a human messenger?' It means that I have not claimed to be God or to share in God's sovereignty for you to make such considerations of me. My Lord is exalted and free from such affiliations. I am nothing but a man and a messenger of God. My role as a messenger is to deliver God's revelation to you. It is not within my power to perform even one of these feats. (Tadabbur-e-Qur'an 4/542)

Additionally, verse 60 of Surah Al-Isra indicates that Allah did not intend in the final prophecy to use miracles and extraordinary signs as a means of warning and instilling fear as was done with certain previous prophets. This is elaborated upon in the following verse from Surah Al-Isra:

وَمَا مَنَعَنَا أَنْ نُّرْسِلَ بِالْآيْتِ اِلَّا أَنْ كَذَّبَ بِهَا الْاَوَّلُوْنَ ۚ وَاٰتَيْنَا ثَمُوْدَ النَّاقَةَ مُبْصِرَةً فَظَلَمُوْا بِهَا ۚ وَمَا نُرْسِلُ بِالْآيْتِ اِلَّا تَخْوِيْفًا .

What has stopped Us from sending signs of punishment is that the earlier generations had denied them. We had given the Thamūd a she-camel [in a similar way] as an eye-opening sign but they were unjust to themselves and denied it. [What then is the use to send signs?] We only send signs to frighten [people before punishing them]. (17:59)

The interpretation provided in *Al-Bayan* states:

It means that when people do not regard (God's signs) with awe but grow even more obstinate and dismiss them, what purpose do these signs serve in being sent? Experience has shown that to warn or to intimidate such obstinate individuals is futile. They are only liable to be influenced by the actual infliction of punishment. (3/94)

This explanation makes it entirely clear that the Qur'an's stance is that the nature of miracles, their occurrence, and the reactions or demands of the direct recipients of prophethood have no intrinsic connection with one another. Therefore, relating these aspects to one another or attempting to understand them in interrelation is incorrect.

Following this, let us now examine the accounts provided in the relevant narrations. As for what has been recorded in the *Sahihain* (Bukhari and Sahih Muslim), there is no ambiguity in those reports.

The narration in Bukhari is:

قال ابو سلمة: سمعت جابر بن عبد الله رضى الله عنهما، قال: سمعت النبى
صلى الله عليه وسلم يقول: لما كذبتنى قريش قمت فى الحجر، فجلى الله لى
بيت المقدس، فطفقت اخبرهم عن آياته وانا انظر إليه.

*Abu Salamah narrates that he heard from Jabir bin Abdullah
(may Allah be pleased with him), who reported from the Prophet
(PBUH), that he said: 'When the Quraysh rejected me regarding
the matter of Isra, I was standing at the Hijr (the area near the
Kaaba). Allah brought Bayt al-Maqdis before me, and I began
describing its signs to them as I looked at it.' (No. 4710)*

And in Muslim:

عن ابى هريرة، قال: قال رسول الله صلى الله عليه وسلم: لقد رايتنى فى الحجر،
وقريش تسالنى عن مسراى، فسالتنى عن اشياء من بيت المقدس لم اثبتها.
فكربت كربةً ما كربت مثله قط، قال: فرفعه الله لى انظر إليه ما يسالونى عن
شىء، إلا انباتهم به.

*Abu Huraira (RA) narrated that the Messenger of Allah
(PBUH) said: 'I saw that I was in the Hijr (the area near the
Kaaba), and the Quraysh were questioning me about my journey.
They asked me about various things concerning Bayt al-Maqdis,
but I was unable to answer them. This caused me such distress as
I had never experienced before. Then Allah lifted Bayt al-
Maqdis before me, and I began to look at it. I described to them
whatever they asked about.' (No. 448)*

The narrations only describe the reaction of the disbelievers from
Quraysh; there is no record of Muslims turning apostate. The reports
that do speak of apostasy do not fulfill the criteria for authenticity as
per scholars and specialists in hadith. Hence, the majority of the
knowledgeable companions rejected these accounts. Maulana Syed
Sulaiman Nadvi has thoroughly and respectfully analyzed these issues
in *Seerat-un-Nabi*. He suggests that certain narratives lack proper
chains of transmission (isnad), and among the narrators are those
known for storytelling and dishonesty. After discussing the incident

cited in the collections of Bukhari and Muslim, he comments:

The story has been documented to this point in the Sahihain (Bukhari and Muslim). However, relating to this event, narrators like Waqidi, Ibn Ishaq, Ibn Jarir Tabari, Ibn Abi Hatim, Bayhaqi, and Hakim, who are not considered authoritative in the tradition literature, have added peculiar annotations. A report from Umm Hani indicates that in the morning, after telling his family about the night's experience, the Prophet planned to share it with others, but she grabbed his clothing and said, 'Do not pursue this, for the disbelievers will categorically deny it.' Another account states when the Prophet wasn't found in his bed at night, his family worried the Quraysh might have hurt him and searched for him in mountains and caves. There is also an account of the Prophet, during his return from the Mi'raj, encountering a Quraysh caravan and subsequent interactions. When the event was denied by the people, the Prophet remarked, 'Alright, your caravan will arrive the day after tomorrow; you can ask them.' Accordingly, when the caravan arrived, they confirmed the Prophet's words. Among these accounts, one states that some disbelievers approached Abu Bakr Siddiq, informing him that Muhammad was proclaiming in the Kaaba about his night journey to Jerusalem and back. Abu Bakr Siddiq inquired if Muhammad had indeed stated this, and upon confirmation, he stated, 'Then I deem him truthful; I believe in it.' The disbelievers questioned, 'How do you believe such an improbable tale?' He responded, 'I believe in things more extraordinary than this - that he receives revelations from angels every day.' Following this, Abu Bakr was known by the title as-Siddiq (The Truthful).

Nevertheless, all these anecdotes are considered utterly frivolous and baseless. Ibn Ishaq and Ibn Saad didn't provide any chains of narration for these events. In contrast, narrators like Ibn Jarir Tabari, Bayhaqi, Ibn Abi Hatim, Abu Ya'la, Ibn Asakir, and Hakim did provide chains for their stories. Among their narrators are individuals such as Abu Ja'far al-Razi, Abu

Harun al-'Abdi, and Khalid ibn Yazid ibn Abi Malik. The first, despite being considered reliable, has a reputation for reporting unfounded hadiths, while the others are notorious for their deception and storytelling.

The final strand of these dubious narratives is the claim that many Muslims had their faith shattered and apostatized upon hearing the Prophet's description of the Mi'raj incident. 'Many who had embraced faith turned away' (Seerat Ibn Hisham 1/241). This narrative likely sprang from a misguided interpretation of the Qur'anic verse: Wa mā Ja'alnā al-ru'yā allatī araynāka illā Fitnatan lilnās (Al-Isra 60), which implies, 'The vision We showed you was only a test for the people.'

Ibn Sa'd and Waqidi have narrated this account without any chain of transmission. Historians such as Tabari, Ibn Abi Hatim, Bayhaqi, and others have cited it referencing the same three associates whose virtues we have recounted earlier. In his commentary on this particular verse, Ibn Jarir has relayed anecdotes from Hasan, Qatada, and Ibn Zaid concerning the defection, but these accounts don't trace back beyond these individuals. The compelling argument against the occurrence of this event lies in the fact that at that time in Mecca, there were only a limited number of companions who had embraced Islam, each known by name. Not one of them has the stain of renouncing Islam. It is possible that among those who previously did not exhibit intense hostility towards the Prophet—even if they did not acknowledge him as the Messenger, they did not accuse him of being untruthful or fabricating lies. However, following the event of the Isra and Mi'raj, they could have forsaken even their favorable inclination and trust towards him. The Holy Qur'an refers to this as 'Fitnatan lilnās' (a trial for mankind), not 'Fitnatan lilmu'mineen' (a trial for the believers or Muslims). Moreover, even if it was a test for the faithful, nothing within this verse indicates that they failed to endure it.

The Concept of Seeing Allah Almighty

The expressions from Surah Al-Najm, *Thumma Danā Fatadallā Fa-kāna qāba qawsayni aw adnā*, and the text from the hadith of the Isra and *Mi'raj, Wa Danā Lil Jabbāri Rabbil Izzati, Fatadallā, Hattā Kāna Minhu Qāba Qawsayni Aw Adnā* are understood to be depicting the vision of the Almighty. The relevant passages regarding this divine vision from the Surah and the hadith are as follows:

وَالنَّجْمِ اِذَا هَوٰى. مَا ضَلَّ صَاحِبُكُمْ وَمَا غَوٰى. وَمَا يَنْطِقُ عَنِ الْهَوٰى. اِنْ هُوَ اِلَّا وَحْىٌ يُوْحٰى. عَلَّمَهٗ شَدِيْدُ الْقُوٰى. ذُوْ مِرَّةٍ فَاسْتَوٰى. وَهُوَ بِالْاُفُقِ الْاَعْلٰى. ثُمَّ دَنَا فَتَدَلّٰى. فَكَانَ قَابَ قَوْسَيْنِ اَوْ اَدْنٰى. فَاَوْحٰى اِلٰى عَبْدِهٖ مَا اَوْحٰى. مَا كَذَبَ الْفُؤَادُ مَا رَاٰى. اَفَتُمٰرُوْنَهٗ عَلٰى مَا يَرٰى.

The stars, when they fall, bear witness that your companion is neither lost nor has he gone astray. He does not speak out of his own fancy. This [Qur'an] is but a revelation sent down to him. He has been taught by one mighty in power, towering in character and endued with wisdom. Thus, he appeared such that he was on the higher horizon. Then he drew near and bent down until he was within two bows' length or even closer. God then revealed to His servant that which He revealed. Whatever he saw was not his heart's delusion. Then will you now quarrel with him over what he is seeing with his eyes? (53:1-12)

ثم علا به فوق ذلك بما لا يعلمه إلا الله، حتى جاء سدرة المنتهى، ودنا للجبار رب العزة، فتدظلى، حتى كان منه قاب قوسين او ادنى، فاوحى الله فيما اوحى إليه خمسين صلاةً على امتك كل يوم وليلة.

Then Gabriel (AS) took the Prophet (PBUH) beyond even the seventh heaven, to those exalted heights that only Allah knows. Until the Prophet (peace and blessings be upon him) reached Sidrat al-Muntaha. Then Allah, the Lord of Glory and Majesty, descended and came near to him, so much so that there remained a distance of two bow-lengths or even closer. Then Allah conveyed His revelation to the Prophet (PBUH), in which fifty prayers were enjoined upon him to be performed every day and night, which were made obligatory upon your Ummah. (Sahih Bukhari, No. 7517)

There are two principal views among scholars regarding the interpretation of seeing the Almighty.

One school of thought maintains that it is incorrect to assert the possibility of a visionary encounter with the Divine in relation to the Prophet (PBUH). Asserting such contradicts Qur'anic verses and hadiths that negate the potentiality of seeing Allah Almighty. Consequently, they contend that the mentioned segment of Surah Al-Najm pertains to the sight of Gabriel (AS). In terms of the tradition which expounds on Allah Almighty's appearance explicitly, some from this group outright dismiss this section of the tradition, while others reject the entire tradition.

Syed Abul A'la Maududi has elaborated on this viewpoint extensively. The following excerpts are from his exegesis of Surah Al-Najm in *Tafheem al-Qur'an*:

Some interpret 'mighty in power' to refer directly to Allah Almighty, but the vast consensus among exegetes identifies it as Gabriel (AS). This view is reported from Abdullah ibn Mas'ud, Aisha, Abu Huraira (may Allah be content with them), Qatada, Mujahid, and Rabe' ibn Anas. Ibn Jarir, Ibn Kathir, Razi, Alusi and others have also upheld this interpretation. Prominent scholars such as Shah Waliullah and Maulana Ashraf Ali Thanvi have echoed this stance in their translations. The most sensible deduction, indeed, aligns with other explicit statements found within the Holy Qur'an itself. ...

This particular verse details the second encounter between Gabriel (AS) and the Prophet (PBUH), during which Gabriel manifested in his true form. The encounter site is pinpointed as

'Sidrat al-Muntaha,' and it is denoted that 'Jannat al-Mawa' is situated adjacent to it. ...

The verse concludes that the Messenger of Allah (PBUH) did not behold Allah Almighty but instead His sublime signs. As the context suggests, this second meeting is with the same entity as the first encounter. Therefore, it is essential to accept that the figure the Prophet witnessed on the utmost horizon initially wasn't Allah, and the one seen near the Sidrat al-Muntaha subsequently wasn't Allah either. If the Prophet had beheld Allah Almighty at any point, it would have constituted an incident of such magnitude that it would undoubtedly have been distinctly conveyed here. ...

For these reasons, it would seem that there should be no room for debate over whether the Messenger of Allah (PBUH) saw Allah Almighty on these two occasions or whether he saw Gabriel (AS). However, the reason this discussion arose is the presence of differing reports in the narrations of Hadith on this matter. ...

A report from Anas bin Malik (RA), which Imam Bukhari has included in the book of Tawheed regarding the incident of Mi'raj and attributed to Shareek bin Abdullah, encounters a significant objection because it contradicts the Qur'an explicitly. This is because the Qur'an details two separate events of vision, one that initially occurred at the highest horizon and then the 'Dana Fatadallā Fa Kana Qāba Qawsayni Aw Adna' episode, and the other happened near Sidrat al-Muntaha. But this report conflates these two events into a single vision. Therefore, since it contradicts the Qur'an, it is unacceptable. (5/195-205)

Hafiz Salahuddin Yusuf has gathered the statements of scholars who believe that Allah Almighty was not seen (by the Prophet during the Mi'raj) in his book *Waqia-e-Mi'raj aur Uske Mushahadat*. He writes:

In some narrations, it is reported solely from Abdullah Ibn Abbas (RA) that the Messenger of Allah (PBUH) saw Allah with his physical eyes. However, on the other hand, it is also reported from Ibn Abbas (RA) that the Messenger of Allah (PBUH) saw Allah with his heart. ...Thus, both types of narrations—seeing with the eyes and seeing with the heart—are transmitted from Ibn Abbas (RA). For this reason, Hafiz Ibn Kathir states:

'The narration of absolute vision from Ibn Abbas (RA) should be interpreted in light of the report specifying vision with the heart, and whoever has conveyed from him about seeing with eyes has said something very odd because such a thing is not substantiated from the companions.'

Contemporary scholar, Nasir al-Din Albani says:

'Regardless, the interpretation of verses of Al-Najm related to the vision of Allah Almighty by Hazrat Ibn Abbas (RA) is affirmed, but the interpretation we mentioned earlier from Prophet Muhammad (PBUH), narrated by Aisha (RA), is preferable. Therefore, it is compulsory to accept the marfu (statement of the Prophet) over the mawqoof (statement of a companion).'

Hafiz Ibn Hajar also notes:

'General narrations concerning vision from Ibn Abbas (RA) and specific ones about vision with the heart exist. So, the general should be interpreted in the light of the specific.'

In summation, from this discussion, it is evident that Prophet Muhammad (PBUH) neither saw Allah nor spoke directly to Him on the night of Mi'raj, nor did he experience the 'approach and drawing near' with Allah, which some have suggested in their explanation of the verses from Surah Al-Najm.' (75-77, 84)

Esteemed scholars from the other viewpoint reconcile the words of Surah Al-Najm *Thumma Danā Fatadallā Fa-kāna qāba qawsayni aw adnā* (Then he approached and drew closer, until he was at a distance of two bow's length or even closer) and the specific statement found in the narrations that says Prophet Muhammad (PBUH) saw

Allah. They support their belief by citing other narrations that explicitly mention seeing Allah. They believe not just in the divine vision, but also interpret the Qur'anic verses *Lā Tudrikuhu al-Absār* and *Wa Mā Kāna Li-Basharin An Yukallimahu Allahu Illā Wahyan Aw Min Warā'i Hijāb* through the lens of these hadiths.

Pir Karam Shah Al-Azhari documented the positions of scholars who advocate the vision of Allah Almighty in his exegesis *Zia ul Qur'an*. His summary is as such:

> *The summary of the discussion is expressed by Allama Nawawi in these words:*
>
> *'The conclusion of the matter is that, according to the majority of scholars, the preferred opinion is that the Messenger of Allah (PBUH) saw Allah Almighty with the eyes of his head during the Night of Ascension, and there is no room for doubt in this.'*
>
> *Allama Syed Mahmood Alusi Baghdadi, after completing the interpretation and explanation of these verses, expresses his personal opinion about the vision of Allah as follows:*
>
> *'I say that the Leader of the Worlds (PBUH) was blessed with the vision of his Noble Lord and was granted closeness to Allah. However, it was in a manner befitting His majestic grandeur.' (Ruh al-Ma'ani)*
>
> *When Imam Ahmad bin Hanbal was asked whether the Prophet (PBUH) had seen his Lord, he would reply: 'Yes, the Prophet (PBUH) saw Allah Almighty, yes, the Prophet (PBUH) saw Allah Almighty.' He would repeat this statement so many times that he would become breathless. (Ruh al-Ma'ani)*
>
> *Mawlana Syed Anwar Shah, after an elaborate discussion on this matter, writes:*
>
> *The Prophet (PBUH) was honored with the vision of Allah. Allah Almighty granted him this eternal blessing and dignified him with His grace and favor. Thus, the Prophet (PBUH) saw*

Allah, the Prophet (PBUH) saw Allah, as Imam Ahmad has said. However, this vision was such as a beloved sees his beloved— not being able to close his eyes, nor having the strength to gaze fixedly at the face of the Beloved. This is the meaning of Allah's statement: 'The sight did not swerve, nor did it transgress.' (Fayd al-Bari, Sharh Fath al-Bari)

Sheikh Abdul Haq Muhaddith Dehlvi, while investigating this issue in the fourth volume of Ashiat-ul-Lam'at, preferred the same opinion that the Holy Prophet (PBUH) was honored with the vision of Allah Almighty. (5/23-24)

In summary, there has been a difference of opinion regarding the sighting of the Divine from the time of the Companions until the present day. One group affirms that the Prophet (PBUH) saw Allah, and another denies it.

In the view of the respected teacher, Javed Ahmed Ghamidi, according to the Qur'an and hadith, both of these viewpoints are incorrect. Behind both lies the same mistake, which is their refusal to accept the events of *Isra* and *Mi'raj* as a dream (*ru'ya*). This refusal contradicts the clear meanings of Verse 60 of Surah Al-Isra, and the explicit words of the hadith in Sahih Bukhari. Both of these sources clearly establish that the event of *Mi'raj* took place not in a state of wakefulness, but in sleep and in the form of a visionary experience. Surah Al-Isra mentions:

$$...وَمَا جَعَلْنَا الرُّءْيَا الَّتِي أَرَيْنَاكَ إِلَّا فِتْنَةً لِّلنَّاسِ...$$

...The dream We showed you We made it a trial too for these people...

And the beginning and ending words of the Hadith are:

حتى اتوه ليلةً اخرى فيما يرى قلبه، وتنام عينه، ولا ينام قلبه، وكذلك الانبياء تنام اعينهم ولا تنام قلوبهم.

واستيقظ وهو فى مسجد الحرام.

Until one other night, they (once again) came. At that time, the state of the Prophet (PBUH) was such that his eyes were asleep, but his heart was not. This is the way with messengers: (even when in a state of sleep,) their eyes may sleep, but their hearts do not.

After this, when the Prophet (PBUH) woke up, he was in Masjid al-Haram.

Therefore, according to Javed Ahmed Ghamidi, it is entirely plausible that during the event of *Mi'raj*, the Messenger of Allah (PBUH) was granted the honor of beholding Allah Almighty. This is also supported by some other narratives suggesting that the Messenger of Allah (PBUH) had the privilege of beholding Allah in a dream state. In Tirmidhi it is stated:

عن معاذ بن جبل رضى الله عنه، قال: احتبس عنا رسول الله صلى الله عليه وسلم ذات غداة عن صلاة الصبح حتى كدنا نتراءى عين الشمس، فخرج سريعًا فثوب بالصلاة فصلى رسول الله صلى الله عليه وسلم وتجوز فى صلاته، فلما سلم دعا بصوته، فقال لنا: على مصافكم كما انتم. ثم انفتل إلينا، ثم قال: اما إنى ساحدثكم ما حبسنى عنكم الغداة انى قمت من الليل فتوضات وصليت ما قدر لى، فنعست فى صلاتى حتى استثقلت فإذا انا بربى تبارك وتعالى فى احسن صورة. فقال: يا محمد، قلت: لبيك رب، قال: فيم يختصم الملا الاعلى؟ قلت: لا ادرى، قالها ثلاثًا، قال: فرايته وضع كفه بين كتفى حتى وجدت برد انامله بين ثديى، فتجلى لى كل شىء وعرفت.

Mu'adh bin Jabal (RA) narrates that one morning the Messenger of Allah (PBUH) delayed leading us in the Fajr prayer. (That is, he did not come, and we refrained from praying while waiting for him.) It was nearly time for us to see the sun (meaning the time of sunrise was very near). Then the Prophet (PBUH) quickly returned and called the people for prayer. He led the prayer and kept it brief. After completing the prayer, he called out to the people and said, 'Sit in your places.'

Then he turned toward us and said, 'I want to tell you what held me back this morning. I woke up during the night, performed ablution, and offered the Tahajjud prayer—just as much as was destined for me. Then, while I was still in prayer, I dozed off, and soon I fell into a deep sleep. All of a sudden, I saw myself in the presence of my Lord, and He was in the best form.'

He said, 'O Muhammad!' I replied, 'My Lord, I am present.' He said, 'Do you know what the angels of the higher assembly are discussing?' I replied, 'I do not know.' Allah asked this question three times. Then the Prophet (PBUH) said, 'I saw Allah. He placed His hand between my shoulders, and I felt the coolness of His fingers in my chest. With that, everything became illuminated before me, and I came to know (everything).' (No. 3235)

Since the narrative of *Mi'raj* explicitly mentions that the Messenger of Allah (PBUH) observed the Divine being in a dream state, it cannot contradict the texts of the Holy Qur'an which reject the possibility of visual sighting of the Divine. Furthermore, by interpreting the observations of *Isra* and *Mi'raj* as visions, in accordance with the explicit words of the Qur'an and Hadith, the following hadith of Aisha (RA), is also completely clarified, and it resolves any perceived contradictions between the narratives of Divine vision:

عن مسروق، قال: كنت متكئًا عند عائشة، فقالت: يا ابا عائشة، ثلاث من تكلم بواحدة منهن، فقد اعظم على الله الفرية، قلت: ما هن؟ قالت: من زعم ان محمدًا صلى الله عليه وسلم راى ربه، فقد اعظم على الله الفرية. قال: وكنت متكئًا فجلست، فقلت: يا ام المؤمنين، انظريني ولا تعجليني، الم يقل الله عز و جل: وَلَقَدْ رَآهُ بِالْأُفُقِ الْمُبِينِ[64] وَلَقَدْ رَآهُ نَزْلَةً أُخْرَى.[65] فقالت: انا اول هذه الامة، سال عن ذلك رسول الله صلى الله عليه وسلم،

---

[64] Surah Al-Takwir 81:23
[65] Surah Al-Najm 53:13

فقال: إنما هو جبريل، لم اره على صورته التى خلق عليها، غير هاتين المرتين، رايه مهبطًا من السماء، سادًا عظم خلقه ما بين السماء إلى الارض. فقالت: اولم تسمع ان الله يقول: لَا تُدْرِكُهُ الْأَبْصَارُ وَهُوَ يُدْرِكُ الْأَبْصَارَ وَهُوَ اللَّطِيفُ الْخَبِيرُ [66] اولم تسمع ان الله يقول: وَمَا كَانَ لِبَشَرٍ أَنْ يُكَلِّمَهُ اللَّهُ إِلَّا وَحْيًا أَوْ مِنْ وَرَائِ حِجَابٍ أَوْ يُرْسِلَ رَسُولًا فَيُوحِيَ بِإِذْنِهِ مَا يَشَاءُ. [67]

Masrooq narrates that I was sitting, reclining on a cushion, at the house of Aisha (RA). Aisha said, 'O Abu Aisha (this was Masrooq's kunya), 'There are three things, and whoever claims any of them has fabricated a great lie against Allah.' I asked, 'What are those three things?' She said, '(One of them is) that someone thinks Muhammad (PBUH) saw his Lord. Such a person has fabricated a great lie against Allah.'

Masrooq said, I was reclining (semi-lying down), and upon hearing this, I immediately sat up. Then I said, 'O Mother of the Believers, please wait and do not rush. Did Allah not say: 'And indeed, he saw him at the clear horizon' and 'And he certainly saw him in another descent'?

Aisha (RA) replied, 'I was the first in this Ummah to ask the Messenger of Allah (PBUH) about these verses.' The Prophet (PBUH) said, 'It was Gabriel (mentioned in these verses). I saw him in his original form only on these two occasions. I saw him descending from the heavens, and his vast form filled the space from the heavens to the earth.'

Then Aisha (RA) said, Have you not heard that Allah says: 'Vision perceives Him not, but He perceives [all] vision; and He is the Subtle, the Acquainted', and 'It is not for any human being that Allah should speak to him except by revelation, or from

---

behind a veil, or by sending a messenger to reveal, by His permission, what He wills'?

Summary of Discussions

The Traditional Position

The key points of our traditional position are as follows:

1. The incident of *Isra* and *Mi'raj* has been mentioned in both the Holy Qur'an and the hadiths. The Qur'an mentions it in summary, and the Hadiths in detail. The event is referred in Surah Al-Isra and Surah Najm of the Qur'an. The event has been reported through about 25 different chains and is quoted in most books of hadith, including Bukhari and Muslim.

2. By connecting the relevant parts of the Qur'an and hadith, the picture that emerges suggests that it is more plausible to regard it as an event that took place on a single occasion. This journey is likely to have begun at night from Masjid al-Haram, proceeded to Masjid Al-Aqsa, and from there, on to the highest heaven, where it was completed.

3. The Prophet (PBUH) experienced this event in a state of wakefulness, and he observed the Divine signs (ayat) both with his physical eye and with the eye of his heart.

4. Indeed, there is no explicit description in the Qur'an and hadith of the Ascension (*Mi'raj*) and the journey being a physical experience in a state of wakefulness. However, the linguistic expressions used in both the Qur'an and Hadith suggest the physical nature of the event and that it took place while the Prophet Muhammad (PBUH) was awake.

5. Although the Holy Qur'an mentions this incident as a *ru'ya*, commonly understood as a dream, it is not appropriate to interpret this journey solely as a spiritual experience or a vision. This is due to several reasons:

i. The word *ru'ya* is mostly used in the sense of a dream. However, it is not exclusive to this meaning. It is also used in the sense of seeing with open eyes. The evidence for this is that renowned Arabic poets like Al-Mutanabbi and Al-Ra'i have used this word in their poetry to mean seeing in a state of wakefulness.

ii. The statement of Abdullah ibn Abbas (RA) is that in Surah Al-Isra, the word *ru'ya* refers to *ru'yatu 'ayn* —that is, seeing with the eyes

iii. In verse 1 of Surah Al-Isra, before narrating this incident, the word *Subhān (Glory be to Him)* is used. This linguistic style necessitates that an extraordinary event is mentioned afterward that highlights Allah's power. This manifestation of Allah's power becomes evident when a journey that would take forty days is completed within a few moments of the night.

iv. In verse 1 of Surah Al-Isra, the words *Alladhī asra bi 'abdihi* (Who took His servant by night) are used. The word *asra* means 'to take someone along,' which is an act that can only be performed with a physical being. Thus, it cannot be applied to a dream.

v. In *Alladhī Asra bi 'abdihi*, the word *abd* (servant) cannot be applied to the soul alone because *abd* refers to a combination of both body and soul. Therefore, the use of this word necessitates that the reference here is to a physical being, which is a composite of body and soul.

vi. In Surah Al-Isra, verse 60, this event is referred to with the words *Fitnatan Lilnās* (a trial for the people). This means that this event was made a test for the people. A trial or test, evidently, can only be caused by something extraordinary. Even the greatest event seen in a dream is not considered extraordinary. Thus, it is impossible that the Prophet (PBUH) narrated a dream, and it became a trial for the people. This trial could only occur if the event was considered a physical occurrence.

vii. It is narrated in hadiths that when the account of this event was shared, people refused to believe it. The disbelievers mocked it, and some Muslims even apostatized. This reaction of the people proves that it was considered a physical journey because if it had been a dream, it would have been considered a normal occurrence and ignored. Neither would the deniers have rejected it, nor would it have led to Muslims turning away from Islam.

The Position of Javed Ahmed Ghamidi

Javed Ahmed Ghamidi presents the following key points:

1. The details presented under the title of *Isra* and *Mi'raj* are not about a single event but rather four distinct events. Among these[68]:

   - The first is the *Event of Isra*, which is mentioned in Surah Al-Isra. This occurred in the realm of a dream.

   - The second is the *Event of Sidra*, mentioned in Surah Al-Najm, verses 1 to 12. This occurred in the state of wakefulness.

   - The third is the *Event of Qāba Qawsayn*, which is also recorded in Surah Al-Najm, verses 13 to 18. This too occurred in the state of wakefulness.

   - The fourth is the *Event of Mi'raj*, which is narrated in Sahih Bukhari, Hadith No. 7517, and some other reports. This occurred in the realm of a dream.

2. The separation of these events is evident as they are depicted individually in the Qur'an and hadith and not presented as a single consolidated event.

3. All four events are divine in origin and should be viewed as signs from Allah. Their very nature is linked to revelation and

---

[68] This is merely the sequence of narration; it should not be interpreted as a chronological order.

inspiration, and the information and experiences described are related to the prophetic mission of the Prophet Muhammad (PBUH). They should be interpreted and understood within this framework.

4. Was the event of *Isra* physical or spiritual? On this matter, the word *al-ru'ya* in Surah Al-Isra, verse 60, holds the status of decisive textual evidence. This means that Allah has not left this matter ambiguous but has explicitly clarified that this event occurred in the realm of dream. Hence, it is necessary to understand the words *Subhān*, *Asra*, and *Abd* in the light of *al-ru'ya*.

5. *Al-ru'ya* is an exceedingly well-known word in the Arabic language. In Arabic, it is used in the sense of seeing in sleep just as we use 'Dream' in English, '*Sapna*' in Hindi, and '*Khwaab*' in Urdu. In the realm of poetry and literature, the meaning of a dream is conveyed using the same word. This is the meaning recorded in Arabic dictionaries. The word appears around seven hundred times in the hadith, and on every occasion, it has been used in this same sense. Even in the Holy Qur'an, the word appears seven times across various chapters, where it always pertains to a dream. If such is the case with the meaning and understanding of this word, then it is essential that in the aforementioned verse, it must be taken to mean a dream, and consequently, the journey of Isra should be understood as a spiritual journey.

6. However, this *Ru'ya* does not refer to the kind of dream that is part of everyday human experience. Absolutely not. This *Ru'ya* is a form of divine revelation (*Wahi Ilahi*) and is exclusive to the prophets. Ordinary humans have no connection with it. Whatever is shown to the prophets in *ru'ya* is truthful, certain, and based on reality. At times, it is even clearer and more evident than seeing something with one's own eyes in a state of wakefulness.

7. With regard to the meaning and understanding *al-Ru'ya*, all arguments advanced by traditional reasoning are contrary to the

Qur'an, hadith, and the principles of language and expression. The points of refutation are as follows:

i. The reference to the poem of Abu Tayyib Al-Mutanabbi regarding the meaning of *ru'ya* is not reliable for the following reasons:

    a. Firstly, the verse (of the Qur'an) does not require one to go outside the Qur'an to Arabic poetry to understand its words or style.

    b. Secondly, there is no commonality in the composition or linguistic style between the verse and the poem. This is because the word *ru'ya* in the verse is used in its literal sense, whereas Al-Mutanabbi has used it in a figurative sense. It is an established linguistic principle that literal and figurative usages cannot serve as evidence for one another.

    c. Thirdly, Al-Mutanabbi is not among the poets whose poetry can be cited as evidence to understand the Qur'an. He was a poet of the Abbasid era and belongs to the fourth category of Arabic poets. However, it is a well-established rule that only the poets of the first two categories can be used as examples to understand the language of the Qur'an and Hadith.

ii. The poem by Al-Ra'i that is cited as evidence also uses the word *ru'ya* in a figurative sense. Since the word in the Qur'anic verse is used in its literal sense, Al-Ra'i's poem cannot be presented as an example.

iii. In the verse under discussion, the word *Subhān* is not used to highlight Allah's power, as is commonly thought. Rather, it is used in the context of Allah being All-Hearing and All-Seeing. The verse begins with *Subhāna alladhī asra bi 'abdihi laylan mina al-masjidi al-harāmi al-masjidi al-aqsa* (Glory be to Him who took His servant by night from the Sacred Mosque to the Farthest Mosque) and ends with *innahu huwa samī'u al-basīr* (Indeed, He is the All-Hearing, the All-Seeing). This means that the context of *Subhān* is determined by *as-samī'u al-basīr*, and the meaning derived is that Allah is far above any suspicion regarding His attributes of hearing and seeing.

iv. Scholars argue that the verb *asra* (to take along) and the noun *abd* (servant) in *alladhī asra bi 'abdihi* refer to the combination of body and soul (a physical being), and therefore, the event must have been a physical journey. This argument contradicts established linguistic principles. It is an accepted fact in every language that the same linguistic structures used for wakeful events are also used for dreams. The only difference is that the dream is explicitly mentioned either before or after the statement. In the Qur'an, the dreams of the Prophet Muhammad (PBUH) (Surah Al-Fath) and Prophet Abraham (PBUH) (Surah Al-Saffat) are described using the same nouns and verbs that are used for wakeful events.

v. Abdullah Ibn Abbas (RA) adopted the phrase *ru'ya 'ayn* to describe the nature of the *Isra* event. This does not mean 'seeing with the eyes,' as is commonly interpreted. Instead, its meaning refers to a dream seen with the eyes. This indicates that the Prophet (PBUH) observed inner, spiritual scenes through physical sight while awake. This interpretation is not inconsistent with the prophetic observations of the Prophet (PBUH), which are well-known and based on reality. For instance, during a solar eclipse prayer, paradise was presented before the Prophet (PBUH), and he reached forward as if to take a cluster of its fruits. Such events may be described as *ru'ya 'ayn* or similar expressions. However, regarding the *Isra* event, despite acknowledging Abdullah ibn Abbas's scholarly stature, the term *ru'ya 'ayn* cannot be applied here, nor can it be taken as a wakeful event. This is because Allah Himself has described this event as *ru'ya* (dream). Therefore, interpreting it as *ru'yah basari* (physical sight) or *ru'ya 'ayn* is not permissible. Had the Qur'an not explicitly clarified this, there might have been room to deduce such interpretations based on context and examples.

vi. The argument that the phrase *Fitnatan lilnās* (a trial for the people) in the verse necessitates the occurrence of a miraculous event is also incorrect. This reasoning, like the other arguments, is very weak. The fundamental reasons for this are as follows:

> a. The premise assumes that the disbelievers of Quraysh found such an enigmatic event, either on a human scale or in association with Prophet Muhammad (PBUH), to be unfathomable. This assumption is flawed as their superstitious beliefs led them to attribute supernatural abilities to their ancestors and deities. Consequently, they had fabricated the charge of the Prophet (PBUH) being, God forbid, a sorcerer or soothsayer. Thus, the extraordinary or confounding nature of an event was not a potential source of their bewilderment.

> b. When Prophet Muhammad (PBUH) recounted the particulars of the Masjid Al-Aqsa to the assembly on the following morning, any reservations held by the disbelieving Quraysh should have dissipated instantly. However, they persisted in their denial of the event, which suggests that the *Fitnatan lilnās* is disconnected from the event's supernatural aspect.

> c. Fundamentally, the argument acknowledges the pretext of the disbelieving Quraysh, which is unsubstantiated by either the verse's language or the historical narrative. It implies that the disbelievers would not have deemed the event a trial had they observed the Prophet (PBUH) ascending to the heavens. The reality remains that in spite of witnessing numerous miracles, their faith was not awakened.

> d. The experience and observation that solely the

Messenger of Allah (PBUH) had, whether it was in the world of dreams or the state of wakefulness, was only of the status of his own narration to people. Therefore, from this perspective, both states (dream and wakefulness) held the same significance for them.

e. In the last sentence of verse 60, Allah Almighty Himself has interpreted the words *Fitnatan lilnās*. After this, there is no room left for conjecture or presenting far-fetched interpretations. It is said, *Wa Nukhawwifuhum Famā Yazīduhum Illā Tugh'yānan Kabīrā* (We only frighten them with the consequences, but it only increases them in great rebellion). Meaning, the thing which has caused the trial is not whether the matter is supernatural or not, but the fear of the consequences. The words *Nukhawwifuhum* stand as the decisive evidence on this.

vii. Rebutting the clear evidence of language and expression through the reactions of people is wrong, both rationally and traditionally. Hence, historical stories in this matter are not worthy of attention. However, despite this, it should be clear that all the traditions relating to apostasy regarding the event of Isra are considered weak and rejected in the view of Hadith scholars.

Appendices

Appendix 1 : Analysis of the Chains of Narratives about *Mi'raj*

Numerous *Marfu* (directly attributed) narrations regarding the event of *Mi'raj* are recorded in the books of Hadith. Among the *Sihah Sittah* (the six authentic collections), these narrations have been transmitted by Bukhari, Muslim, Tirmidhi, Nasa'i, and Ibn Majah. However, they are not mentioned in the *Muwatta* of Imam Malik and the *Sunan of Abu Dawood*. The primary narrator of these narrations is Anas Ibn Malik (RA). In some versions, he narrates directly from the Messenger of Allah (PBUH), while in others, he transmits through Abu Dharr Ghifari (RA) and Malik bin Sa'sa'ah (RA). If the chains of transmission (Asanid) of these narrations are examined in the mentioned books, the following representative narrations can be identified:

1. Bukhari, Hadith No. 7517

Sulaiman (*Tābi' Tābi'i* - Follower of Follower) → Shareek bin Abdullah (*Tābi'i* - Follower) → Anas bin Malik (RA) (Companion) → Messenger of Allah (PBUH)

2. Bukhari, Hadith No. 349

Yunus (*Tābi' Tābi'i*) → Ibn Shihab al-Zuhri (*Tābi'i*) → Anas bin Malik (RA) (Companion) → Abu Dharr Ghifari (RA) (Companion) → Messenger of Allah (PBUH)

3. Bukhari, Hadith No. 3887

Hammam bin Yahya (*Tābi' Tābi'i*) → Qatadah (*Tābi'i*) → Anas bin Malik (RA) (Companion) → Malik bin Sa'sa'ah (RA) (Companion) → Messenger of Allah (PBUH)

4. Muslim, Hadith No. 429

Hammad bin Salamah (*Tābi' Tābi'i*) → Thabit al-Bunani (*Tābi'i*) → Anas bin Malik (RA) (Companion) → The Messenger of Allah (PBUH)

5. Muslim, Hadith No. 433

Yunus (*Tābi' Tābi'i*) → Ibn Shihab al-Zuhri (*Tābi'i*) → Anas bin Malik (RA) (Companion) → Abu Dharr Ghifari (RA) (Companion) → Messenger of Allah (PBUH)

6. Muslim, Hadith No. 434

Saeed (*Tābi' Tābi'i*) → Qatadah (*Tabi'i*) → Anas bin Malik (RA) (Companion) → Malik bin Sa'sa'ah (RA) (Companion) → The Messenger of Allah (PBUH)

7. Tirmidhi, Hadith No. 3346

Saeed (*Tābi' Tābi'i*) → Qatadah (*Tābi'i*) → Anas bin Malik (RA) (Companion) → Malik bin Sa'sa'ah (RA) (Companion) → The Messenger of Allah (PBUH)

8. Ibn Majah, Hadith No. 1399

Yunus bin Yazid (*Tābi' Tābi'i*) → Ibn Shihab al-Zuhri (*Tābi'i*) → Anas bin Malik (RA) (Companion) → The Messenger of Allah (PBUH)

9. Nasa'i, Hadith No. 448

Hisham Dastuwa'i (*Tābi' Tābi'i*) → Qatadah (*Tābi'i*) → Anas bin Malik (RA) (Companion) → Malik bin Sa'sa'ah (RA) (Companion) → The Messenger of Allah (PBUH)

In these nine narratives, the narrators include six Followers of Followers (*Tābi' Tābi'i*), four Followers (*Tābi'i*), and three Companions. The four Followers who have narrated these hadiths are:

    a.   Shareek bin Abdullah

b. Ibn Shihab al-Zuhri

c. Qatadah

d. Thabit al-Bunani

These four Followers are not narrating from different companions but from the same companion, Anas bin Malik (RA). As a necessary consequence of this fact, it is essential to accept two realities:

The first is that, in essence, this is one narration transmitted from Anas bin Malik (RA). From him, it was further narrated by four different narrators. That is, it is one hadith which has been reported through four different chains.

Secondly, the differences that have emerged in its text are possibly the result of errors, forgetfulness, omissions, or additions by the followers (*Tabi'een*) or the narrators after them. This is because it is very unlikely for a credible narrator to relate an incident in such a way that it is contradictory or varies within itself. That is, it is inconceivable for any rational and intelligent person to, for example, describe a single event as both a dream and a wakeful experience at the same time.

In this context, when we compare the aforementioned chains of transmission, one chain appears to differ from the others in terms of the core events. This is the chain of Thabit al-Bunani, which has been narrated by Muslim. That is, the narrations of Shareek bin Abdullah, Ibn Shihab al-Zuhri, and Qatadah in Bukhari share a general similarity, whereas the narration of Thabit al-Bunani in Muslim is different from them. This difference is evident in terms of both omissions and additions. In the three narrations of Bukhari, the incident of the splitting of the chest (*Shaq al-Sadr*) is mentioned, whereas in the narration of Muslim, there is neither any mention of it nor any indication toward it. Similarly, the journey to Masjid Al-Aqsa is not part of the event in the three narrations of Bukhari, while in the narration of Muslim, the event begins with this journey. Based on this analysis, it seems reasonable to conclude that the original event is the one transmitted by Shareek bin Abdullah, Ibn Shihab al-Zuhri, and Qatadah. In contrast, the narration transmitted by Thabit al-Bunani appears to contain certain inaccuracies.

Furthermore, Thabit al-Bunani's narrative highlights a departure and discrepancy from the incident of *Isra* mentioned in the Qur'an. This is because, in the Qur'an, only the event of *Isra*, i.e., the journey from Masjid Al-Haram to Masjid Al-Aqsa, is described. The celestial journey of *Mi'raj* is not included with it, while in Thabit al-Bunani's narration, both these journeys are combined and recounted. Other narrations do not pose this problem of non-conformity with the Qur'an, as they do not mention the event of *Isra* at all.

Another noteworthy point is that aside from Sahih Muslim, no other hadith compiler among the Sahih books has transmitted Thabit al-Bunani's narration. In *Sunan an-Nasa'i*, however, a narration on the same subject, No. 450, has been transmitted by Yazid bin Abi Malik from Anas bin Malik (RA). Nonetheless, this narration has been deemed *munkar* (rejected) by Nasir al-Din Albani.[69]

Based on these detailed considerations, it is most prudent to suspend judgment on some parts of the narration recorded by Thabit al-Bunani in Muslim, considering them a result of his or some subsequent narrator's error, forgetfulness or additions, and to derive the details of the event of *Mi'raj* from other narrations.

---

[69]*Sahih wa Da'if Sunan an-Nasa'i*, Al-Maktabah al-Shamilah. A *Munkar* (rejected) hadith is one in which a weak narrator appears in the chain, and the narration contradicts the narration of a reliable (*thiqa*) narrator. According to the scholars of Hadith, a *Munkar* hadith is considered extremely weak.

Appendix 2 : Comparative Review of Narratives about *Mi'raj*

In Appendix 1, most of the narratives from the Sahih books referenced are those that detail the event extensively. In addition to these, there are also shorter narrations that describe the same event partially. Among the mentioned narrations, some texts are brief, while others are more comprehensive. This demonstrates that the narrators transmitted what they understood, what they remembered, and what they considered significant according to their own comprehension, memory, and discretion, using their own words.[70]

However, apart from the narration of Thabit al-Bunani, the remaining narrations show a general level of agreement and consistency. Despite this, differences in the details, diversity in expressions, and variations in the length or brevity of the narrations cannot be denied. Below is a comparative analysis of their contents.

The Presence of the Prophet

- In five narratives , it is clearly stated that the Prophet (PBUH) was present at Al-Masjid Al-Haram.

- In two narratives, it is mentioned that he was resting in his home.

- In two narratives, there is no mention.

Conclusion: Whether the Prophet (PBUH) was present in Al-Masjid Al-Haram or at home, either scenario is possible. There is a difference in the narrations regarding this detail. However, this difference does not affect the essence of the event. In our view, since the majority of narrations explicitly mention Al-Masjid Al-Haram, this account

---

[70] It should be clear that in this method of *riwayah bil-ma'na* (narration by meaning), every narrator in the chain of transmission adopts the same approach. As a result, by the time a narration reaches Bukhari, Muslim, and other Hadith scholars, differences and variations occur among its different transmission routes.

should be considered closer to reality.

Dream or Wakefulness

- None of these narratives explicitly mention being awake or a physical *Mi'raj*.

- However, one narrative specifies sleep and a spiritual *Mi'raj*.

- Three narratives describe a state between sleep and wakefulness.

Conclusion: There is no disagreement or contradiction in the narrations regarding this matter. That is, it is not the case that some narrations mention wakefulness while others mention sleep. In this context, if some narrations explicitly state sleep, then it must necessarily be accepted. The reason for this is that it is an established principle of knowledge and reasoning that when an event is transmitted by multiple narrators, its details should be determined by reconciling and analyzing all the narrations together.

Splitting of the Chest

- There is a consensus among the narrations that Gabriel (AS) arrived alongside other angels.

- The narratives also concur that Gabriel (AS) split open the chest of the Prophet (PBUH), cleansed his internal cavity with Zamzam water, and then imbued it with faith and wisdom before closing it up again.

Summary: There is no contradiction in any of the aforementioned accounts regarding this matter; thus, there is no reason to reject their authenticity. Furthermore, since the incident occurred within the realm of a dream, it does not lead to any difficulties in comprehension.

Riding the Buraq

- The riding of Buraq is mentioned in four narratives, while remaining unmentioned in others.

Conclusion: The concept of a lightning-speed mount is not

implausible. All narratives are harmonious regarding this subject. Therefore, accepting this account is entirely appropriate. Moreover, since the event is portrayed as happening within the realm of a dream, its symbolic interpretation is entirely possible.

Observing the Al-Aqsa Mosque

- One account states that prior to ascending on the *Mi'raj*, Prophet Muhammad (PBUH) visited the Al-Aqsa Mosque.

- Other accounts suggest that he ascended to the heavens directly from Masjid al-Haram.

Conclusion: From the details and analysis presented in Appendix 1, it is evident that only the narration of Thabit al-Bunani includes the addition of the journey to Masjid Al-Aqsa. The other narrations do not mention this. It is known that the journey to Masjid Al-Aqsa, i.e., the *Isra* event, is mentioned in the Qur'an as a separate incident, and it does not include the journey to the heavens. Furthermore, even those narrations in which Allah presented Masjid Al-Aqsa as a representation before the Prophet (PBUH) do not mention the heavenly journey.[71] Based on this, it seems most accurate to conclude that the mention of the journey to Masjid Al-Aqsa was inadvertently included by the narrator. It is a separate event and is not directly related to the heavenly journey of *Mi'raj*.

Ascension to the Heavens with Gabriel (AS)

- Every narrative confirms that Gabriel (AS) was responsible for escorting the Prophet to the heavens.

- Apart from the audience in the Divine Presence, he remained with the Prophet (PBUH) throughout the entire journey.

---

[71] We are referring to the incident when the Messenger of Allah (PBUH) informed the people about the event of, and they mocked his words. Then, in their gathering, he described all the details of the journey. On this occasion, Allah Almighty, to facilitate him, presented *Masjid al-Aqsa* before him in a represented form, and he continued describing its structure to them.

Conclusion: There is no disagreement in the hadiths concerning the Prophet Muhammad's (PBUH) ascension to the celestial realms accompanied by Gabriel (AS). Neither reason nor textual evidence opposes this, and therefore, this account should be accepted as accurate.

Entry into Each of the Seven Heavens

- All accounts narrate that Prophet Muhammad (PBUH) traveled sequentially through all seven heavens.

- He witnessed various phenomena on each of the heavens.

Conclusion: The tour through the seven heavens is also consistent with reason and tradition. No conflicting accounts have been reported regarding this. As such, its veracity should be accepted.

Meetings with Various Prophets in the Heavens

- The Prophet Muhammad (PBUH) encountered one divine prophet on each of the heavens.

- All accounts unanimously describe the meeting with Prophet Adam (PBUH) on the first heaven.

- The names of the prophets with whom the encounters took place are largely consistent across the narratives.

- Although there exist minor differences concerning which prophet was met on which heaven, these do not affect the factuality of the encounters.

Conclusion: We cannot determine the precise nature of the encounters with various prophets in the different heavens. Nonetheless, it should be acknowledged that these were spiritual encounters for two main reasons: firstly, if the Prophet Muhammad (PBUH) was in a spiritual state during the vision, then the prophets he met would also be in a comparable spiritual state. Secondly, as the prophets are to remain without their physical bodies until the Day of Judgment due to their demise, it seems unlikely that these encounters were corporeal.

Observing the Sidrat al-Muntaha

- The observation of *Sidrat al-Muntaha* is mentioned in five narrations, while it is not mentioned in the rest.

Conclusion: In Surah Al-Najm, it is stated that Prophet Muhammad (PBUH) witnessed *Sidrat al-Muntaha* with his own eyes and also saw Gabriel (AS) in that place, while he [the Prophet] was still on Earth. This makes it abundantly clear that *Sidrat al-Muntaha* is indeed a real entity. However, this incident has no direct relation to the *Mi'raj* event as explained in the narrations. Thus, the observation of *Sidrat al-Muntaha* during *Mi'raj* should be regarded as a distinct event. Additionally, the difference lies in the manner of observation; the one in the Qur'an was with open eyes, whereas the one in the hadiths happened in a state of a dream.

Proximity to the Divine and the Vision of the Almighty

- One of the narratives emphasizes that the Almighty granted Prophet Muhammad (PBUH) an extraordinary closeness, described as *Qāba Qawsayn* meaning that the distance between Allah and the Prophet (PBUH) was no greater than two bow lengths. Naturally, such proximity suggests a dream.

- No such explicit detail is mentioned in other traditions.

Conclusion: It is conveyed in some traditions that Prophet Muhammad (PBUH) beheld Allah in the realm of dream, making the occurrence quite credible. Although some Qur'anic verses and traditions dismiss the possibility of seeing Allah with the naked eye, the visionary experiences during *Mi'raj* are unrelated to the open-eyed vision, and therefore, do not conflict with Qur'an or hadith.

The Commandment of Fifty Prayers and the Advice of Prophet Moses (PBUH)

- All narratives unanimously state that Allah initially mandated fifty prayers each day. When the Prophet (PBUH) conveyed this directive, Prophet Moses (PBUH) suggested that he request a reduction in the number from Allah.

- The narratives are also consistent in describing how the Prophet (PBUH) repeatedly sought an audience with Allah to reduce the number, eventually bringing back the final commandment of five daily obligatory prayers.

Conclusion: The act of *Salah* (prayer) has been a fundamental pillar in the religion of Allah. It is clearly stated in the Qur'an that Allah prescribed *Salah* to all prophets and their people. In *Sunan Abi Dawud*, No. 393, there is mention of Gabriel (AS) enlightening Prophet Muhammad (PBUH) about the five daily prayers having been a continual practice. Hence, the most logical conclusion would be that *Salah* was established from the beginning of the Prophet's mission, and the realities related to its establishment were presented symbolically during *Mi'raj*.

Appendix 3 : Narrative of Yunus from Anas ibn Malik (RA)

Bukhari, No. 349

حدثنا يحيى بن بكير، قال: حدثنا الليث، عن يونس، عن ابن شهاب، عن انس بن مالك، قال: كان ابو ذر يحدث، ان رسول الله صلى الله عليه وسلم، قال: فرج عن سقف بيتي وانا بمكة، فنزل جبريل صلى الله عليه وسلم ففرج صدري، ثم غسله بماء زمزم، ثم جاء بطست من ذهب ممتلئ حكمةً وإيمانًا، فافرغه فى صدري، ثم اطبقه، ثم اخذ بيدي فعرج بى إلى السماء الدنيا.

فلما جئت إلى السماء الدنيا، قال جبريل لخازن السماء: افتح، قال: من هذا؟ قال: هذا جبريل، قال: هل معك احد؟ قال: نعم، معى محمد صلى الله عليه وسلم، فقال: ارسل إليه؟ قال: نعم، فلما فتح علونا السماء الدنيا، فإذا رجل قاعد على يمينه اسودة وعلى يساره اسودة، إذا نظر قبل يمينه ضحك وإذا نظر قبل يساره بكى، فقال: مرحبًا بالنبى الصالح والابن الصالح، قلت لجبريل: من هذا؟ قال: هذا آدم، وهذه الاسودة عن يمينه وشماله نسم بنيه، فاهل اليمين منهم اهل الجنة والاسودة التى عن شماله اهل النار؟ فإذا نظر عن يمينه ضحك، وإذا نظر قبل شماله بكى. حتى عرج بى إلى السماء الثانية، فقال لخازنها: افتح، فقال له خازنها مثل ما قال الاول، ففتح.

قال انس: فذكر انه وجد فى السموات آدم وإدريس وموسى وعيسى وإبراهيم صلوات الله عليهم، ولم يثبت كيف منازلهم، غير انه ذكر انه وجد آدم فى السماء الدنيا، وإبراهيم فى السماء السادسة.

قال انس: فلما مر جبريل بالنبى صلى الله عليه وسلم بإدريس، قال: مرحبًا بالنبى الصالح والاخ الصالح، فقلت: من هذا؟ قال: هذا إدريس، ثم مررت بموسى، فقال: مرحبًا بالنبى الصالح والاخ الصالح، قلت: من هذا؟ قال:

هذا موسى، ثم مررت بعيسى، فقال: مرحبًا بالاخ الصالح والنبى الصالح،
قلت: من هذا؟ قال: هذا عيسى. ثم مررت بإبراهيم، فقال: مرحبًا بالنبى
الصالح والابن الصالح، قلت: من هذا؟ قال هذا إبراهيم عليه وسلم.

قال ابن شهاب: فاخبرنى ابن حزم، ان ابن عباس، وابا حبة الانصارى كانا
يقولان: قال النبى صلى الله عليه وسلم: ثم عرج بى حتى ظهرت لمستوّى
اسمع فيه صريف الاقلام، قال ابن حزم، وانس بن مالك: قال النبى صلى
الله عليه وسلم: ففرض الله على امتى خمسين صلاةً.

فرجعت بذلك حتى مررت على موسى، فقال: ما فرض الله لك على امتك؟
قلت: فرض خمسين صلاةً، قال: فارجع إلى ربك، فإن امتك لا تطيق ذلك،
فراجعت فوضع شطرها. فرجعت إلى موسى، قلت: وضع شطرها، فقال:
راجع ربك، فإن امتك لا تطيق، فراجعت: فوضع شطرها، فرجعت إليه،
فقال: ارجع إلى ربك فإن امتك لا تطيق ذلك، فراجعته، فقال: هى خمس
وهى خمسون لا يبدل القول لدى.

فرجعت إلى موسى فقال: راجع ربك، فقلت: استحييت من ربى، ثم انطلق
بى حتى انتهى بى إلى سدرة المنتهى، وغشيها الوان لا ادرى ما هى، ثم
ادخلت الجنة فإذا فيها حبايل اللؤلؤ وإذا ترابها المسك.

Yahya bin Bukair narrated to us, saying: Al-Layth narrated to us, from Yunus, from Ibn Shihab, from Anas bin Malik (RA), who said: Abu Dharr al-Ghifari (RA) used to narrate that the Prophet (PBUH) said: 'The roof of my house was opened while I was in Makkah, and Gabriel (AS) descended. He split my chest, then washed it with the water of Zamzam. After that, he brought a golden tray filled with wisdom and faith, poured its contents into my chest, and then sealed it. Then he took my hand and ascended with me to the heavens.'

When we reached the first heaven, Gabriel (AS) said to the gatekeeper of the heaven, 'Open.' The gatekeeper asked, 'Who is this?' Gabriel (AS) replied, 'This is Gabriel.' The gatekeeper asked, 'Is anyone with you?'

Gabriel (AS) said, 'Yes, Muhammad (PBUH) is with me.' The gatekeeper asked, 'Has he been sent for?' Gabriel (AS) replied, 'Yes.' When the gate was opened, we ascended to the first heaven. There, we saw a man sitting with a multitude of people on his right and a multitude on his left. When he looked to his right, he smiled, and when he looked to his left, he wept. He welcomed me and said, 'Welcome, O righteous Prophet and righteous son!' I asked Gabriel, 'Who is this?' He replied, 'This is Adam (PBUH), and the multitudes on his right and left are the souls of his children. Those on the right are the people of Paradise, and those on the left are the people of Hell. When he looks to his right, he smiles, and when he looks to his left, he weeps.'

Then Gabriel ascended with me to the second heaven and said to its gatekeeper, 'Open.' The gatekeeper asked the same questions as the first, and then he opened the gate.

Anas (RA) said that Abu Dharr (RA) mentioned that the Prophet (PBUH) saw Adam, Idris, Musa, Isa, and Abraham (PBUH) in the heavens. Abu Dharr (RA) did not mention the specific locations of all of them, except that he said the Prophet (PBUH) found Adam (PBUH) on the first heaven and Abraham (PBUH) on the sixth heaven.

Anas (RA) narrated that when Gabriel (AS) passed by Idris (PBUH) with the Prophet (PBUH), Idris (PBUH) said, 'Welcome, O righteous Prophet and righteous brother!' I asked Gabriel, 'Who is this?' He replied, 'This is Idris (PBUH).'

Then we passed by Musa (PBUH), who said, 'Welcome, O righteous Prophet and righteous brother!' I asked Gabriel, 'Who is this?' He replied, 'This is Musa (PBUH).'

Then we passed by Isa (PBUH), who said, 'Welcome, O righteous Prophet and righteous brother!' I asked Gabriel, 'Who is this?' He replied, 'This is Isa (PBUH).'

Then we passed by Abraham (PBUH), who said, 'Welcome, O righteous Prophet and righteous son!' I asked Gabriel, 'Who is this?' He replied, 'This is Abraham (PBUH).'

Ibn Shihab said that Abu Bakr bin Hazm informed me that Abdullah bin Abbas (RA) and Abu Habba al-Ansari (RA) used to say: The Prophet (PBUH) said, 'Then Gabriel ascended with me until we reached a level where I could hear the creaking of the pens (which was the sound of the pens of the angels' writings).'

Ibn Hazm and Anas bin Malik (RA) narrated that the Prophet (PBUH) said: 'Then Allah made fifty prayers obligatory upon my Ummah'.

I descended with this command and passed by Musa (PBUH). He asked, 'What has Allah made obligatory for your Ummah?' I replied, 'Fifty prayers.' He said, 'Return to your Lord, for your Ummah will not be able to bear this.' So I returned to my Lord, and He reduced it by half.

When I returned to Musa (PBUH), I informed him, and he said, 'Go back to your Lord, for your Ummah cannot bear this.' I kept going back and forth between my Lord and Musa (PBUH) until Allah said, 'They are five prayers, but they are equal to fifty (in reward). My word does not change.'

I returned to Musa (PBUH), and he again said, 'Go back to your Lord.' But I replied, 'I feel shy before my Lord now.'

Then Gabriel (RA) took me to Sidrat al-Muntaha, which was covered in colors that I do not know. After that, I was taken into Paradise, where I saw strings of pearls, and its soil was of musk.

Appendix 4 : Narrative of Hammam bin Yahya from Anas ibn Malik

Bukhari, No. 3887

حدثنا هدبة بن خالد، حدثنا همام بن يحيى، حدثنا قتادة، عن انس بن مالك، عن مالك بن صعصعة رضى الله عنهما، ان نبى الله صلى الله عليه وسلم حدثهم، عن ليلة اسرى به قال: بينما انا فى الحطيم، وربما قال: فى الحجر، مضطجعًا إذ اتانى آت فقد، قال: وسمعته يقول فشق ما بين هذه إلى هذه، فقلت للجارود وهو إلى جنبى: ما يعنى به، قال: من ثغرة نحره إلى شعرته وسمعته يقول: من قصه إلى شعرته فاستخرج قلبى، ثم اتيت بطست من ذهب مملوءة إيمانًا فغسل قلبى، ثم حشى.

ثم اتيت بدابة دون البغل وفوق الحمار ابيض، فقال له الجارود: هو البراق يا ابا حمزة، قال انس: نعم يضع خطوه عند اقصى طرفه.

فحملت عليه فانطلق بى جبريل حتى اتى السماء الدنيا فاستفتح، فقيل: من هذا؟ قال: جبريل، قيل: ومن معك؟ قال: محمد، قيل: وقد ارسل إليه، قال: نعم، قيل: مرحبًا به فنعم المجىء جاء. ففتح فلما خلصت فإذا فيها آدم، فقال: هذا ابوك آدم فسلم عليه، فسلمت عليه فرد السلام، ثم قال: مرحبًا بالابن الصالح، والنبى الصالح.

ثم صعد بى حتى اتى السماء الثانية فاستفتح، قيل: من هذا؟ قال: جبريل، قيل ومن معك؟ قال محمد، قيل: وقد ارسل إليه، قال: نعم، قيل: مرحبًا به فنعم المجىء جاء، ففتح، فلما خلصت إذا يحيى وعيسى وهما ابنا الخالة، قال: هذا يحيى، وعيسى فسلم عليهما، فسلمت فردا، ثم قالا: مرحبًا بالاخ الصالح والنبى الصالح.

ثم صعد بى إلى السماء الثالثة فاستفتح، قيل: من هذا؟ قال: جبريل، قيل
ومن معك؟ قال: محمد، قيل: وقد ارسل إليه، قال: نعم، قيل: مرحبًا به فنعم
المجىء جاء، ففتح، فلما خلصت إذا يوسف، قال: هذا يوسف فسلم عليه،
فسلمت عليه فرد، ثم قال: مرحبًا بالاخ الصالح والنبى الصالح.

ثم صعد بى حتى اتى السماء الرابعة فاستفتح، قيل: من هذا؟ قال: جبريل،
قيل: ومن معك؟ قال: محمد، قيل: اوقد ارسل إليه، قال: نعم، قيل: مرحبًا
به فنعم المجىء جاء، ففتح، فلما خلصت إلى إدريس، قال: هذا إدريس فسلم
عليه، فسلمت عليه فرد، ثم قال: مرحبًا بالاخ الصالح والنبى الصالح.

ثم صعد بى حتى اتى السماء الخامسة فاستفتح، قيل: من هذا؟ قال: جبريل،
قيل: ومن معك؟ قال: محمد، قيل: وقد ارسل إليه، قال: نعم، قيل: مرحبًا
به فنعم المجىء جاء، فلما خلصت فإذا هارون، قال: هذا هارون فسلم
عليه، فسلمت عليه فرد، ثم قال: مرحبًا بالاخ الصالح والنبى الصالح.

ثم صعد بى حتى اتى السماء السادسة فاستفتح، قيل: من هذا؟ قال: جبريل،
قيل: من معك؟ قال: محمد، قيل: وقد ارسل إليه، قال: نعم، قال: مرحبًا به فنعم
المجىء جاء، فلما خلصت فإذا موسى، قال: هذا موسى فسلم عليه، فسلمت
عليه فرد، ثم قال: مرحبًا بالاخ الصالح والنبى الصالح، فلما تجاوزت بكى،
قيل: له ما يبكيك، قال: ابكى لان غلامًا بعث بعدى يدخل الجنة من امته
اكثر ممن يدخلها من امتى.

ثم صعد بى إلى السماء السابعة فاستفتح جبريل، قيل: من هذا؟ قال: جبريل،
قيل: ومن معك؟ قال: محمد، قيل: وقد بعث إليه؟ قال: نعم، قال: مرحبًا به
فنعم المجىء جاء، فلما خلصت فإذا إبراهيم، قال: هذا ابوك فسلم عليه، قال:
فسلمت عليه فرد السلام، قال: مرحبًا بالابن الصالح والنبى الصالح.

ثم رفعت إلى سدرة المنتهى، فإذا نبقها مثل قلال هجر وإذا ورقها مثل آذان
الفيلة، قال: هذه سدرة المنتهى وإذا اربعة انهار: نهران باطنان، ونهران

ظاهران، فقلت: ما هذان يا جبريل، قال: اما الباطنان فنهران فى الجنة،
واما الظاهران فالنيل، والفرات، ثم رفع لى السبت المعمور، ثم اتيت بإناء
من خمر، وإناء من لبن، وإناء من عسل، فاخذت اللبن، فقال: هى الفطرة
التى انت عليها وامتك.

ثم فرضت على الصلوات خمسين صلاةً كل يوم، فرجعت فمررت على موسى،
فقال: بما امرت، قال: امرت بخمسين صلاةً كل يومٍ، قال: إن امتك لا تستطيع
خمسين صلاةً كل يومٍ، وإنى والله قد جربت الناس قبلك وعالجت بنى
إسرائيل اشد المعالجة، فارجع إلى ربك فاساله التخفيف لامتك، فرجعت
فوضع عنى عشرًا.

فرجعت إلى موسى فقال مثله، فرجعت فوضع عنى عشرًا، فرجعت إلى
موسى فقال مثله، فرجعت فوضع عنى عشرًا فرجعت إلى موسى، فقال مثله،
فرجعت فامرت بعشر صلوات كل يوم، فرجعت فقال مثله، فرجعت فامرت
بخمس صلوات كل يوم.

فرجعت إلى موسى، فقال: بم امرت، قلت: امرت بخمس صلوات كل يوم،
قال: إن امتك لا تستطيع خمس صلوات كل يوم وإنى قد جربت الناس قبلك
وعالجت بنى إسرائيل اشد المعالجة، فارجع إلى ربك فاساله التخفيف
لامتك، قال: سالت ربى حتى استحييت ولكنى ارضى واسلم، قال: فلما
جاوزت نادى مناد امضيت فريضتى وخففت عن عبادى.

*Narrated by Hudbah bin Khalid: He said, Hammad bin
Yahya narrated to us, from Qatadah, from Anas bin Malik
(RA), from Malik bin Sa'sa'ah (RA), who said that the Prophet
Muhammad (PBUH) narrated to them the incident of Laylat
al-Mi'raj (the Night of Ascension). The Prophet (PBUH) said:*

*'I was lying in Hatim'—sometimes Qatadah said Hajr instead
of Hatim—'when someone came to me (Gabriel, AS) and split
my chest open.' Qatadah narrated that I heard Anas (RA) say,*

'From here to here.' I asked Jarood, who was sitting nearby, what Anas (RA) meant by this phrase. He explained, 'He meant from the throat to the navel.' Qatadah also said, 'I heard Anas (RA) narrate that the Prophet's chest was split open from the upper chest to the navel.' Then my heart was removed, and a golden tray filled with faith and wisdom was brought. My heart was washed and filled with this content, and then it was returned to its place.

After that, a white animal was brought, smaller than a horse and larger than a donkey. Jarood asked Anas (RA), 'O Abu Hamzah, was it the Buraq?' Anas replied, 'Yes, it was. Its every stride reached as far as it could see.'

The Prophet (PBUH) continued: 'I was mounted on it, and Gabriel (AS) took me until we reached the sky of this world.' Gabriel (AS) asked for the gate to be opened. A voice asked, 'Who is this?' Gabriel (AS) replied, 'It is Gabriel.' The voice asked, 'Is anyone with you?' Gabriel (AS) replied, 'Yes, Muhammad (PBUH) is with me.' The voice asked, 'Have you been sent to bring him?' Gabriel (AS) replied, 'Yes.' Then the voice welcomed me: 'Welcome! What an excellent arrival this is!' The gate was opened, and when I entered, I saw Adam (PBUH). Gabriel (AS) said, 'This is your father, Adam (PBUH). Greet him.' I greeted him, and he returned the greeting, saying, 'Welcome, O righteous son and righteous Prophet!'

Then Gabriel (AS) took me upward to the second heaven and asked for the gate to be opened. A voice asked, 'Who is this?' Gabriel (AS) replied, 'It is Gabriel.' The voice asked, 'Is anyone with you?' Gabriel (AS) replied, 'Yes, Muhammad (PBUH) is with me.' The voice asked, 'Have you been sent to bring him?' Gabriel (AS) replied, 'Yes.' Then the voice welcomed me: 'Welcome! What an excellent arrival this is.' The gate was opened, and when I entered, I found John and Jesus (PBUH), who were maternal cousins. Gabriel (AS) said, 'These are John and Jesus (PBUH). Greet them.' I greeted them, and they *returned the greeting, saying, 'Welcome, O righteous Prophet and righteous brother!'*

Then Gabriel (AS) took me to the third heaven and asked for the gate to be opened. A voice asked, 'Who is this?' Gabriel (AS) replied, 'It is Gabriel.' The voice asked, 'Is anyone with you?' Gabriel (AS) replied, 'Yes, Muhammad (PBUH) is with me.' The voice asked, 'Have you been sent to bring him?' Gabriel (AS) replied, 'Yes.' Then the voice welcomed me: 'Welcome! What an excellent arrival this is!' The gate was opened, and when I entered, I found Joseph (PBUH). Gabriel (AS) said, 'This is Joseph (PBUH). Greet him.' I greeted him, and he returned the greeting, saying, 'Welcome, O righteous Prophet and righteous brother!'

Then Gabriel (AS) took me to the fourth heaven and asked for the gate to be opened. A voice asked, 'Who is this?' Gabriel (AS) replied, 'It is Gabriel.' The voice asked, 'Is anyone with you?' Gabriel (AS) replied, 'Yes, Muhammad (PBUH) is with me.' The voice asked, 'Have you been sent to bring him?' Gabriel (AS) replied, 'Yes.' Then the voice welcomed me: 'Welcome! What an excellent arrival this is!' The gate was opened, and when I entered, I met Idris (PBUH). Gabriel (AS) said, 'This is Idris (PBUH). Greet him.' I greeted him, and he returned the greeting, saying, 'Welcome, pure brother and noble prophet!'

Then Gabriel (AS) took me to the fifth heaven and asked for the gate to be opened. A voice asked, 'Who is this?' Gabriel (AS) replied, 'It is Gabriel.' The voice asked, 'Is anyone with you?' Gabriel (AS) replied, 'Yes, Muhammad (PBUH) is with me.' The voice asked, 'Have you been sent to bring him?' Gabriel (AS) replied, 'Yes.' Then the voice welcomed me: 'Welcome! What an excellent arrival this is!' The gate was opened, and when I entered, I met Aaron (PBUH). Gabriel (AS) said, 'This is Aaron (PBUH). Greet him.' I greeted him, and he returned the greeting, saying, 'Welcome, O righteous Prophet and righteous brother!'

Then Gabriel (AS) took me to the sixth heaven and asked for the gate to be opened. A voice asked, 'Who is this?' Gabriel (AS) replied, 'It is Gabriel.' The voice asked, 'Is anyone with you?' Gabriel replied, 'Yes, Muhammad (PBUH) is with me.' The voice asked, 'Have you been sent to bring him?' Gabriel (AS) replied, 'Yes.' Then the voice welcomed me: 'Welcome! What an excellent arrival this is!' The gate was opened, and when I entered, I met Moses (PBUH). Gabriel (AS) said, 'This is Moses (PBUH). Greet him.' I greeted him, and he returned the greeting, saying, 'Welcome, O righteous Prophet and righteous brother!' When I moved forward, Moses (PBUH) began to cry. He was asked, 'What makes you weep?' He replied, 'I am weeping because this young man has been sent as a Prophet after me, but his followers will enter Paradise in greater numbers than my followers.'

Then Gabriel (AS) took me to the seventh heaven and asked for the gate to be opened. A voice asked, 'Who is this?' Gabriel (AS) replied, 'It is Gabriel.' The voice asked, 'Is anyone with you?' Gabriel (AS) replied, 'Yes, Muhammad (PBUH) is with me.' The voice asked, 'Have you been sent to bring him?' Gabriel (AS) replied, 'Yes.' Then the voice welcomed me: 'Welcome! What an excellent arrival this is!' The gate was opened, and when I entered, I found Abraham (PBUH). Gabriel (AS) said, 'This is your father, Abraham (PBUH). Greet him.' I greeted him, and he returned the greeting, saying, 'Welcome, O righteous Prophet and righteous son!'

Then Sidrat al-Muntaha (The Lote Tree at the Farthest Limit) was brought before me. Its fruits were (big) like the pots of Hajr, and its leaves were like the ears of elephants. Gabriel (AS) said, 'This is Sidrat al-Muntaha.' I saw four rivers there—two hidden and two visible. I asked Gabriel, 'What are these rivers?' He said, 'The two hidden ones are rivers of Paradise, and the two visible ones are the Nile and the Euphrates.'

Then al-Bayt al-Ma'mur (the frequently visited house) was

brought before me. A cup of wine, a cup of milk, and a cup of honey were presented to me. I took the cup of milk, and Gabriel (AS) said, 'This is the fitrah (natural disposition), upon which you and your Ummah are.'

Then fifty daily prayers were made obligatory upon me. I returned and came to Moses (PBUH), who asked, 'What has been commanded to you?' I replied, 'I have been ordered fifty daily prayers.' Moses (PBUH) said, 'Your Ummah will not be able to bear this. I have already dealt with people before and have had a bitter experience with the Israelites. Therefore, go back to your Lord and request a reduction for your Ummah.' So, I returned to the presence of Allah and requested a reduction, and ten prayers were reduced.

Upon returning, when I reached Moses (PBUH), he asked the same question (and gave the same advice). Thus, I once again presented myself before Allah's court (and requested a reduction). This time, ten daily prayers were reduced. I then went back to Moses (PBUH), and he repeated his advice. I returned once more to the presence of the Lord Almighty, resulting in a reduction of ten more prayers.

When I reached Moses (PBUH) again, he repeated his advice. I went back once more, and ten more prayers were reduced. This process was repeated again, and I presented myself before the divine court. As a result, the command for five daily prayers was finalized.

After this, when I came to Moses (PBUH), he asked, 'What command has been given now?' I replied, 'The command is for five daily prayers.' He once again gave the same advice and said, 'Your Ummah will not be able to bear even this. I have dealt with people before you and have had a bitter experience with the Israelites. Go to your Lord once more and request further reduction.' The Prophet (PBUH) said, 'I have now repeatedly asked my Lord, and I feel shy to make any further requests.

Therefore, I am content with this.' The Prophet (PBUH) then said, 'As I was about to leave, a voice called out, We have finalized Our command and granted ease to Our servants.'

Appendix 5 : Narrative of Ibn Shihab al-Zuhri from Anas ibn Malik

Muslim, No. 433

وحدثني حرملة بن يحيى التجيبي، اخبرنا ابن وهب، قال: اخبرني يونس، عن ابن شهاب، عن انس بن مالك، قال: كان ابو ذر يحدث، ان رسول الله صلى الله عليه وسلم، قال: فرج سقف بيتي وانا بمكة، فنزل جبريل عليه السلام، ففرج صدري، ثم غسله من ماء زمزم، ثم جاء بطست من ذهب ممتلئ حكمةً وإيمانًا، فافرغها في صدري، ثم اطبقه، ثم اخذ بيدي فعرج بي إلى السماء، فلما جئنا السماء الدنيا، قال جبريل عليه السلام لخازن السماء الدنيا: افتح، قال: من هذا؟ قال: هذا جبريل، قال: هل معك احد؟ قال: نعم، معي محمد صلى الله عليه وسلم، قال: فارسل إليه؟ قال: نعم، ففتح، قال: فلما علونا السماء الدنيا، فإذا رجل عن يمينه اسودة، وعن يساره اسودة، قال: فإذا نظر قبل يمينه ضحك، وإذا نظر قبل شماله بكى، قال: فقال: مرحبًا بالنبي الصالح والابن الصالح، قال: قلت: يا جبريل، من هذا؟ قال: هذا آدم عليه السلام وهذه الاسودة عن يمينه، وعن شماله نسم بنيه، فاهل اليمين اهل الجنة والاسودة التي عن شماله اهل النار، فإذا نظر قبل يمينه ضحك، وإذا نظر قبل شماله بكى.

قال: ثم عرج بي جبريل، حتى اتى السماء الثانية، فقال لخازنها: افتح، قال: فقال له خازنها: مثل ما قال خازن السماء الدنيا، ففتح.

فقال انس بن مالك: فذكر انه وجد في السماوات، آدم، وإدريس، وعيسى، وموسى، وإبراهيم صلوات الله عليهم اجمعين، ولم يثبت كيف منازلهم، غير انه ذكر، انه قد وجد آدم عليه السلام في السماء الدنيا وإبراهيم في السماء السادسة.

قال: فلما مر جبريل ورسول الله صلى الله عليه وسلم بإدريس صلوات الله عليه، قال: مرحبًا بالنبي الصالح والاخ الصالح، قال: ثم مر، فقلت: من هذا؟ فقال: هذا إدريس.

قال: ثم مررت بموسى عليه السلام، فقال: مرحبا بالنبى الصالح والاخ الصالح،

قال: قلت: من هذا؟ قال: هذا موسى.

قال: ثم مررت بعيسى، فقال مرحبًا بالنبى الصالح والاخ الصالح، قلت: من هذا؟

قال: هذا عيسى ابن مريم.

قال: ثم مررت بإبراهيم عليه السلام، فقال: مرحبًا بالنبى الصالح والابن الصالح،

قال: قلت: من هذا؟ قال: هذا إبراهيم.

قال ابن شهاب: واخبرنى ابن حزم، ان ابن عباس وابا حبة الانصارى، كانا

يقولان: قال رسول الله صلى الله عليه وسلم: ثم عرج بى، حتى ظهرت

لمستوًى اسمع فيه صريف الاقلام.

قال ابن حزم وانس بن مالك: قال رسول الله صلى الله عليه وسلم: ففرض

الله على امتى خمسين صلاةً، قال: فرجعت بذلك حتى امر بموسى، فقال

موسى عليه السلام: ماذا فرض ربك على امتك؟ قال: قلت: فرض عليهم

خمسين صلاةً، قال لى موسى عليه السلام: فراجع ربك، فإن امتك لا تطيق

ذلك، قال: فراجعت ربى فوضع شطرها، قال: فرجعت إلى موسى عليه

السلام فاخبرته، قال: راجع ربك، فإن امتك لا تطيق ذلك، قال: فراجعت

ربى، فقال: هى خمس، وهى خمسون لا يبدل القول لدى، قال: فرجعت إلى

موسى، فقال: راجع ربك، فقلت: قد استحييت من ربى.

قال: ثم انطلق بى جبريل، حتى ناتى سدرة المنتهى، فغشيها الوان لا ادرى

ما هى، قال: ثم ادخلت الجنة، فإذا فيها جنابذ اللؤلؤ وإذا ترابها المسك.

*Narrated by Anas bin Malik (RA): Abu Dharr al-Ghifari
(RA) narrated that the Prophet Muhammad (PBUH) said:*

*'I was in Makkah when the roof of my house was opened, and
Gabriel (AS) descended. He split open my chest, washed it with
the water of Zamzam, and brought a golden tray filled with
wisdom and faith. He poured it into my chest and then sealed it.
After that, he took my hand and ascended with me to the nearest*

heaven.'

Gabriel (AS) asked the gatekeeper to open the door. The gatekeeper asked, 'Who is this?' Gabriel (AS) replied, 'It is Gabriel.' The gatekeeper asked, 'Is anyone with you?' Gabriel (AS) replied, 'Yes, Muhammad (PBUH) is with me.' The gatekeeper asked, 'Has he been sent for?' Gabriel (AS) replied, 'Yes.' Then the gate was opened, and we ascended.

On the first heaven, I saw a man surrounded by groups of people on his right and left. When he looked to his right, he smiled, and when he looked to his left, he wept. He greeted me, saying, 'Welcome, O righteous Prophet and righteous son!' I asked Gabriel (AS), 'Who is this?' He replied, 'This is Adam (PBUH), and the groups on his right and left are his children. Those on the right are destined for Paradise, and those on the left are destined for Hell. When he looks to his right, he smiles (with joy), and when he looks to his left, he weeps (with sorrow.)'

The Prophet (PBUH) continued: 'After that, Gabriel (AS) ascended with me to the second heaven. He asked for the gate to be opened, and the same exchange occurred as with the first heaven. Then the gate was opened.'

Anas bin Malik (RA) said: The Prophet (PBUH) met Adam, Idris, Jesus, Moses, and Abraham (PBUH) during the journey through the heavens. However, the Prophet (PBUH) did not mention in detail which Prophet he met on which heaven, except that Adam (PBUH) was on the first heaven and Abraham (PBUH) was on the sixth heaven.

The Prophet (PBUH) continued: When Gabriel (AS) and I reached Idris (PBUH), he greeted me, saying, 'Welcome, O righteous Prophet and righteous brother!' I asked Gabriel (AS), 'Who is this?' He replied, 'This is Idris (PBUH).'

The Prophet (PBUH) continued: Then we reached by Moses (PBUH), who said, 'Welcome, O righteous Prophet and righteous brother!' I asked Gabriel (AS), 'Who is this?' He replied, 'This is Moses (PBUH).'

The Prophet (PBUH) continued: Then we passed by Jesus (PBUH), who said, 'Welcome, O righteous Prophet and righteous brother!' I asked Gabriel (AS), 'Who is this?' He replied, 'This is Jesus (PBUH), the son of Maryam (AS).'

After that, we reached Abraham (PBUH), who said, 'Welcome, O righteous Prophet and righteous son!' I asked Gabriel (AS), 'Who is this?' He replied, 'This is Abraham (PBUH).'

Ibn Shihab said: Ibn Hazm narrated to me that Ibn Abbas (RA) and Abu Hubba al-Ansari (RA) (whether it was Aamir, Malik, or Thabit) used to say that the Prophet (PBUH) said: 'Then I was taken to a high and smooth place where I could hear the sound of pens.'

Ibn Hazm and Anas bin Malik (RA) further narrated that the Prophet (PBUH) said: 'Then Allah made fifty prayers obligatory upon my Ummah.' When I returned, I passed by Moses (PBUH), who asked, 'What has Allah made obligatory upon your Ummah?' I said, 'Fifty prayers.' Moses (PBUH) said, 'Return to your Lord and ask for a reduction, for your Ummah will not be able to bear this.' So I returned to my Lord, and He reduced it by a portion.

On my return, when I came to Musa (AS) and informed him of what had happened, he said, 'Go back to your Lord and request a further reduction, for your Ummah will not be able to bear this.' So I returned to my Lord. Allah Almighty said, 'Five prayers are obligatory, and they are equal to fifty in reward. My decree does not change.' The Prophet (PBUH) said, 'I accepted this command and returned. When I reached Musa (AS), he repeated the same advice and suggested returning to the Lord. To this, I said, 'Now I feel shy to go back to my Lord for this matter again.'

Then Gabriel (AS) took me to Sidrat al-Muntaha. It was covered with colors, the nature of which I do not know. After that, I was taken into Paradise, where I saw domes made of pearls, and its soil was of musk.

Appendix 6 : Narrative of Qatadah from Anas ibn Malik (RA)

Muslim, No. 434

حدثنا محمد بن المثنى، حدثنا ابن ابى عدى، عن سعيد، عن قتادة، عن انس بن مالك لعله، قال: عن مالك بن صعصعة رجل من قومه، قال: قال نبى الله صلى الله عليه وسلم: بينا انا عند البيت بين النائم واليقظان، إذ سمعت قائلاً، يقول: احد الثلاثة بين الرجلين، فاتيت فانطلق بى، فاتيت بطست من ذهب فيها من ماء زمزم، فشرح صدرى إلى كذا وكذا، قال قتادة: فقلت للذى معى: ما يعنى؟ قال: إلى اسفل بطنه، فاستخرج قلبى، فغسل بماء زمزم، ثم اعيد مكانه، ثم حشى إيمانًا وحكمةً.

ثم اتيت بدابة ابيض، يقال له البراق فوق الحمار ودون البغل، يقع خطوه عند اقصى طرفه، فحملت عليه، ثم انطلقنا حتى اتينا السماء الدنيا، فاستفتح جبريل عليه السلام، فقيل: من هذا؟ قال: جبريل، قيل: ومن معك؟ قال: محمد صلى الله عليه وسلم، قيل: وقد بعث إليه؟ قال: نعم، قال: ففتح لنا، وقال: مرحبًا به ولنعم المجىء جاء، قال: فاتينا على آدم عليه السلام.

انه لقى فى السماء الثانية عيسى ويحيى عليها السلام، وفى الثالثة يوسف، وفى الرابعة إدريس، وفى الخامسة هارون، صلوات الله عليهم.

قال: ثم انطلقنا حتى انتهينا إلى السماء السادسة، فاتيت على موسى عليه السلام، فسلمت عليه، فقال: مرحبًا بالاخ الصالح، والنبى الصالح، فلما جاوزته بكى، فنودى ما يبكيك، قال: رب، هذا غلام بعثته بعدى يدخل من امته الجنة اكثر مما يدخل من امتى.

قال: ثم انطلقنا حتى انتهينا إلى السماء السابعة، فاتيت على إبراهيم، وقال فى

الحديث: وحدث نبى الله صلى الله عليه وسلم، انه راى اربعة انهار يخرج من اصلها نهران ظاهران، ونهران باطنان، فقلت: يا جبريل، ما هذه الانهار؟ قال: اما النهران الباطنان فنهران فى الجنة، واما الظاهران فالنيل والفرات.

ثم رفع لى البيت المعمور، فقلت: يا جبريل، ما هذا؟ قال: هذا البيت المعمور، يدخله كل يوم سبعون الف ملك، إذا خرجوا منه لم يعودوا فيه آخر ما عليهم.

ثم اتيت بإناءين احدهما خمر والآخر لبن، فعرضا على فاخترت اللبن، فقيل: اصبت اصاب الله بك امتك على الفطرة.

ثم فرضت على كل يوم خمسون صلاةً، ثم ذكر قصتها إلى آخر الحديث.

Narrated by Anas bin Malik (RA): He likely heard from one of his people, Malik bin Sa'sa'ah (RA), that the Messenger of Allah (PBUH) said:

'I was near the Kaaba, and I was in a state that was between sleep and wakefulness. Suddenly, I heard someone say something as the third among two men who were approaching. Then they came to me and took me away.'

'After that, a golden tray filled with Zamzam water was brought to me. My chest was split open from here to here.' Qatadah said, I asked my companion, What does he mean by 'from here to here'?' He replied, From the throat to below the stomach.

The Prophet (PBUH) continued: 'Then my heart was removed, washed with Zamzam, and returned to its place. It was filled with faith and wisdom.'

Then a white animal, called Buraq, was brought to me. It was taller than a donkey but shorter than a mule, and it placed its step as far as its eye could see. I was mounted on it, and then we set off until we reached the first heaven.

Gabriel (AS) asked for the gate to be opened. The angels asked,

'Who is it?' He replied, 'Gabriel.' They asked, 'Who is with you?' He replied, 'Muhammad (PBUH).' They asked, 'Has he been sent for?' Gabriel (AS) replied, 'Yes.' The gate was then opened, and the angels said, 'Welcome! Your arrival is blessed.' Then we came to Adam (PBUH).

Then the Prophet (PBUH) met Jesus (PBUH) and John (PBUH) on the second heaven. On the third heaven, he met Joseph (PBUH). On the fourth heaven, he met Idris (PBUH). On the fifth heaven, he met Aaron (PBUH).

Then we moved forward until we reached the sixth heaven, where I met Moses (PBUH). I greeted him, and he said, 'Welcome, O righteous brother and righteous Prophet.' As I moved forward, he began to weep. A voice called out, 'O Moses, why are you crying?' He replied, 'O Lord, this young man was sent as a Messenger after me, but his followers will enter Paradise in greater numbers than mine.'

The Prophet (PBUH) continued: 'We then moved forward and reached the seventh heaven, where I saw Abraham (PBUH). Then I saw four rivers flowing from the roots of the Sidrat (Lote Tree). Two of them were hidden, and two were visible.' I asked, 'O Gabriel, what are these rivers?' He replied, 'The hidden ones are rivers of Paradise, and the visible ones are the Nile and the Euphrates.'

Then al-Bayt al-Ma'mur (the frequently visited house) was presented before me. I asked Gabriel (RA), 'What is this?' He replied, 'This is al-Bayt al-Ma'mur. Every day, seventy thousand angels enter it, and they never return. That is the end of their turn.'

Then two vessels were brought before me: one containing wine and the other containing milk. Both were presented to me, and I chose the milk. A voice called out, 'You have chosen correctly. Allah has guided you to the right path, and your Ummah will follow the same path.'

Then fifty daily prayers were made obligatory upon me. The entire account was then narrated until the end.

Appendix 7 : Narrative of Qatadah from Anas ibn Malik (RA)

Nasa'i , No. 448

اخبرنا يعقوب بن إبراهيم، قال: حدثنا يحيى بن سعيد، قال: حدثنا هشام الدستوائي، قال: حدثنا قتادة، عن انس بن مالك عن مالك بن صعصعة ان النبي صلى الله عليه وسلم، قال: بينا انا عند البيت بين النائم واليقظان، إذ اقبل احد الثلاثة بين الرجلين، فاتيت بطست من ذهب ملآن حكمةً وإيمانًا فشق من النحر إلى مراق البطن فغسل القلب بماء زمزم ثم ملئ حكمةً وإيمانًا.

ثم اتيت بدابة دون البغل وفوق الحمار، ثم انطلقت مع جبريل عليه السلام فاتينا السماء الدنيا، فقيل: من هذا؟ قال: جبريل، قيل: ومن معك؟ قال: محمد، قيل: وقد ارسل إليه، مرحبًا به ونعم المجيء جاء، فاتيت على آدم عليه السلام فسلمت عليه، قال: مرحبًا بك من ابن ونبي.

ثم اتينا السماء الثانية، قيل: من هذا؟ قال: جبريل، قيل: ومن معك؟ قال: محمد، فمثل ذلك، فاتيت على يحيى، وعيسى فسلمت عليهما، فقالا: مرحبا بك من اخ ونبي.

ثم اتينا السماء الثالثة، قيل: من هذا؟ قال: جبريل، قيل: ومن معك؟ قال: محمد، فمثل ذلك، فاتيت على يوسف عليه السلام فسلمت عليه، قال: مرحبًا بك من اخ ونبي.

ثم اتينا السماء الرابعة، فمثل ذلك، فاتيت على إدريس عليه السلام فسلمت عليه، فقال: مرحبًا بك من اخ ونبي.

ثم اتينا السماء الخامسة، فمثل ذلك، فاتيت على هارون عليه السلام

فسلمت عليه، قال: مرحبًا بك من اخ ونبى.

ثم اتينا السماء السادسة، فمثل ذلك، ثم اتت على موسى عليه السلام فسلمت عليه، فقال: مرحبًا بك من اخ ونبى، فلما جاوزته بكى، قيل: ما يبكيك؟ قال: يا رب، هذا الغلام الذى بعثته بعدى يدخل من امته الجنة اكثر وافضل مما يدخل من امتى.

ثم اتينا السماء السابعة، فمثل ذلك، فاتيت على إبراهيم عليه السلام، فسلمت عليه، فقال: مرحبًا بك من ابن ونبى.

ثم رفع لى البيت المعمور، فسالت جبريل، فقال: هذا البيت المعمور يصلى فيه كل يوم سبعون الف ملك فإذا خرجوا منه لم يعودوا فيه آخر ما عليهم، ثم رفعت لى سدرة المنتهى فإذا نبقها مثل قلال هجر وإذا ورقها مثل آذان الفيلة وإذا فى اصلها اربعة انهار نهران باطنان ونهران ظاهران، فسالت جبريل، فقال: اما الباطنان ففى الجنة واما الظاهران فالفرات والنيل.

ثم فرضت على خمسون صلاةً فاتيت على موسى، فقال: ما صنعت؟ قلت: فرضت على خمسون صلاةً، قال: إنى اعلم بالناس منك، إنى عالجت بنى إسرائيل اشد المعالجة وإن امتك لن يطيقوا ذلك فارجع إلى ربك فاساله ان يخفف عنك، فرجعت إلى ربى فسالته ان يخفف عنى فجعلها اربعين، ثم رجعت إلى موسى عليه السلام، فقال: ما صنعت؟ قلت: جعلها اربعين، فقال لى مثل مقالته الاولى، فرجعت إلى ربى عز وجل فجعلها ثلاثين، فاتيت على موسى عليه السلام فاخبرته، فقال لى مثل مقالته الاولى، فرجعت إلى ربى فجعلها عشرين ثم عشرةً ثم خمسةً، فاتيت على موسى عليه السلام، فقال لى مثل مقالته الاولى، فقلت: إنى استحى من ربى عز وجل ان ارجع إليه، فنودى ان قد امضيت فريضتى وخففت عن عبادى واجزى بالحسنة عشر امثالها.

Narrated by Anas bin Malik (RA): He narrated from Malik bin Sa'sa'ah (RA) that the Prophet Muhammad (PBUH) said:

I was (resting) near the Kaaba, in a state between sleep and wakefulness, when three individuals came to me. One of them, who was between the other two, came to me. Then a gold tray filled with wisdom and faith was brought to me. He split open my chest from the throat to the lower part of the stomach, took out my heart, and washed it with Zamzam water. Then he filled it with wisdom and faith.

After that, a creature was brought to me, smaller than a mule but larger than a donkey, and I set off with Gabriel (AS). We reached the first heaven. Gabriel asked for the gate to be opened. It was asked, 'Who is it?' Gabriel replied, 'It is Gabriel.' They asked, 'Who is with you?' Gabriel replied, 'Muhammad (PBUH).' They asked, 'Has he been sent for?' When Gabriel confirmed, they said, 'Welcome, his arrival is blessed.' Then I came to Adam (PBUH) and greeted him. He said, 'Welcome, O son and Prophet!'

We then ascended to the second heaven. It was asked, 'Who is it?' Gabriel replied, 'It is Gabriel.' They asked, 'Who is with you?' Gabriel replied, 'Muhammad (PBUH).' They asked, 'Has he been sent for?' The same happened here (as it did on the first heaven). I reached Jesus (PBUH) and John (PBUH). I greeted them, and they said, 'Welcome, O brother and Prophet!'

We then ascended to the third heaven. It was asked, 'Who is it?' Gabriel replied, 'It is Gabriel.' They asked, 'Who is with you?' Gabriel replied, 'Muhammad (PBUH).' They asked, 'Has he been sent for?' The same happened here (as it did on the previous heavens). I met Joseph (PBUH), greeted him, and he said, 'Welcome, O brother and Prophet!'

We ascended to the fourth heaven, where the same occurred (as it did on the previous heavens). I met Idris (PBUH), greeted him, and he said, 'Welcome, O brother and Prophet!'

We then ascended to the fifth heaven. The same exchange took place (as it did on the previous heavens), and I met Aaron

(PBUH). I greeted him, and he said, 'Welcome, O brother and Prophet!'

We ascended to the sixth heaven. The same exchange took place (as it did on the previous heavens), and I met Moses (PBUH). I greeted him, and he said, 'Welcome, O brother and Prophet!' When I moved forward, he began to weep. He was asked, 'Why are you weeping?' Moses (PBUH) replied, 'O Lord, this young man has been sent as a Prophet after me, but his followers will enter Paradise in greater numbers than mine.'

We then ascended to the seventh heaven. The same exchange took place, and I met Abraham (PBUH). I greeted him, and he said, 'Welcome, O son and Prophet!'

Then al-Bayt al-Ma'mur (the frequently visited house) was brought close to me. I asked Gabriel (AS) about it, and he said, 'This is al-Bayt al-Ma'mur. Every day, seventy thousand angels enter it, and when they leave, they never return. That is their final visit.'

Then Sidrat al-Muntaha (The Lote Tree at the Farthest Limit) was brought before me. Its fruits were like clay jugs from Hajar, and its leaves were like the ears of elephants. From its roots flowed four rivers: two hidden and two visible. I asked Gabriel (AS) about these rivers, and he said, 'The hidden rivers are in Paradise, and the visible ones are the Nile and the Euphrates.'

Then fifty daily prayers were made obligatory upon me. During my return journey, I reached Musa (AS), and he asked, 'What did you do?' I replied, 'Fifty prayers have been made obligatory upon me.' He said, 'I know people better than you; I have dealt with Bani Israel. Your Ummah will not be able to bear this. So, return to your Lord and request a reduction.'

I returned to my Lord and requested a reduction, which He granted by decreasing the number to forty. When I went back to Musa (AS), he asked, 'What happened?' I said, 'Allah has reduced the prayers to forty.' He repeated the same advice as before. I again presented myself before my Lord, and He reduced the number to thirty. When I informed Musa (AS), he again said what he had said earlier. So, I returned to my Lord, who then reduced the number to twenty, then to ten, and finally to five.

When I came to Musa (AS) again, he repeated the same advice. I responded, '(Now) I feel shy to go back to my Lord repeatedly.' Then a voice called out, 'I have finalized My command and granted ease to My servants. For each prayer, I will give a tenfold reward.'

Appendix 8 : Narrative of Ibn Shihab al-Zuhri from Anas ibn Malik (RA)

Ibn Majah, No. 1399

حدثنا حرملة بن يحيى المصرى، حدثنا عبد الله بن وهب، اخبرنى يونس بن
يزيد، عن ابن شهاب، عن انس بن مالك، قال: قال رسول الله صلى الله عليه
وسلم: فرض الله على امتى خمسين صلاةً، فرجعت بذلك حتى آتى على موسى،
فقال موسى: ماذا افترض ربك على امتك؟، قلت: فرض على خمسين صلاةً،
قال: فارجع إلى ربك فإن امتك لا تطيق ذلك، فراجعت ربى، فوضع عنى
شطرها، فرجعت إلى موسى فاخبرته: فقال: ارجع إلى ربك فإن امتك لا تطيق
ذلك، فراجعت ربى، فقال: هى خمس، وهى خمسون، لا يبدل القول لدى،
فرجعت إلى موسى، فقال: ارجع إلى ربك، فقلت: قد استحييت من ربى.

*Narrated by Anas bin Malik (RA): The Messenger of Allah
(PBUH) said: Allah Almighty initially made fifty prayers
obligatory upon my Ummah (on the night of Mi'raj). As I was
returning with this command, I passed by Moses (PBUH), who
asked, 'What has your Lord made obligatory upon your
Ummah?' I replied, 'Fifty prayers.' Moses (PBUH) said, 'Go
back to your Lord and request a reduction, for your Ummah will
not be able to bear this.'*

*So, I returned to my Lord, and He reduced the number by half.
I then returned to Moses (PBUH) and informed him (about this
reduction). He said, 'Go back to your Lord again and request
further reduction, for your Ummah will still not be able to bear
this.'*

*So, I went back to my Lord again, and He said, 'They are five
prayers now, but their reward will be equal to fifty. My decree
does not change and is final.'*

After this, I returned to Moses (PBUH), who again said, 'Go back to your Lord and ask for further reduction.' I replied, 'I now feel shy to return to my Lord.'

Appendix 9 : Narrative of Qatadah from Anas Ibn Malik

Tirmidhi, No. 3346

حدثنا محمد بن بشار، حدثنا محمد بن جعفر، وابن أبى عدى، عن سعيد بن
أبى عروبة، عن قتادة، عن انس بن مالك، عن مالك بن صعصعة رجل من
قومه، ان النبى صلى الله عليه وسلم، قال: بينما انا عند البيت بين النائم
واليقظان إذ سمعت قائلاً يقول: احد بين الثلاثة، فأتيت بطست من ذهب
فيها ماء زمزم فشرح صدرى إلى كذا وكذا، قال قتادة: قلت لانس بن مالك:
ما يعنى؟ قال: إلى اسفل بطنى، فاستخرج قلبى فغسل قلبى بماء زمزم ثم
اعيد مكانه ثم حشى إيمانًا وحكمةً، وفى الحديث قصة طويلة.

Narrated by Anas bin Malik (RA): He narrated from a man of his tribe, Malik bin Sa'sa'ah (RA), that the Prophet Muhammad (PBUH) said:

'I was near the House of Allah (Baytullah) in a state between sleep and wakefulness (i.e., in a semi-dream state). Suddenly, I heard someone saying, 'He is one of the three men.' Then a golden tray was brought to me, and it contained Zamzam water. My chest was split open from here to here.'

Qatadah said, I asked Anas (RA), 'From where to where?' He replied, 'The Prophet (PBUH) said: from the throat to below the stomach.'

The Prophet (PBUH) continued: 'My heart was removed, washed with Zamzam water, and then returned to its place. It was filled with faith and wisdom.'

Anas (RA) added: 'This narration contains a lengthy account.'

Appendix 10 : Narrative of Thabit al-Bunani from Anas ibn Malik

Muslim, No. 429

حدثنا شيبان بن فروخ، حدثنا حماد بن سلمة، حدثنا ثابت البناني، عن انس بن مالك، ان رسول الله صلى الله عليه وسلم، قال: اتيت بالبراق وهو دابة ابيض، طويل فوق الحمار، ودون البغل يضع حافره عند منتهى طرفه، قال: فركبته حتى اتيت بيت المقدس، قال: فربطته بالحلقة التى يربط به الانبياء، قال: ثم دخلت المسجد فصليت فيه ركعتين، ثم خرجت، فجاءنى جبريل عليه السلام بإناء من خمر، وإناء من لبن، فاخترت اللبن، فقال جبريل: اخترت الفطرة.

ثم عرج بنا إلى السماء، فاستفتح جبريل، فقيل: من انت؟ قال: جبريل، قيل: ومن معك؟ قال: محمد، قيل: وقد بعث إليه؟ قال: قد بعث إليه ففتح لنا، فإذا انا بآدم فرحب بى، ودعا لى بخير.

ثم عرج بنا إلى السماء الثانية، فاستفتح جبريل عليه السلام، فقيل: من انت؟ قال: جبريل، قيل: ومن معك؟ قال: محمد، قيل: وقد بعث إليه؟ قال: قد بعث إليه ففتح لنا، فإذا انا بابنى الخالة عيسى ابن مريم ويحيى بن زكرياء صلوات الله عليهما، فرحبا ودعوا لى بخير.

ثم عرج بى إلى السماء الثالثة، فاستفتح جبريل، فقيل: من انت؟ قال: جبريل، قيل: ومن معك؟ قال: محمد صلى الله عليه وسلم، قيل: وقد بعث إليه؟ قال: قد بعث إليه ففتح لنا، فإذا انا بيوسف عليه السلام، إذا هو قد اعطى شطر الحسن، فرحب ودعا لى بخير.

ثم عرج بنا إلى السماء الرابعة، فاستفتح جبريل عليه السلام، قيل: من هذا؟ قال: جبريل، قيل: ومن معك؟ قال: محمد، قال: وقد بعث إليه؟ قال:

قد بعث إليه ففتح لنا، فإذا انا بإدريس، فرحب ودعا لى بخير، قال الله عز وجل: وَّ رَفَعۡنٰهُ مَكَانًا عَلِيًّا.

ثم عرج بنا إلى السماء الخامسة، فاستفتح جبريل، قيل: من هذا؟ قال: جبريل، قيل: ومن معك؟ قال: محمد، قيل وقد بعث إليه؟ قال: قد بعث إليه ففتح لنا، فإذا انا بهارون عليه السلام، فرحب ودعا لى بخير.

ثم عرج بنا إلى السماء السادسة، فاستفتح جبريل عليه السلام، قيل: من هذا؟ قال: جبريل، قيل: ومن معك؟ قال: محمد، قيل: وقد بعث إليه؟ قال: قد بعث إليه ففتح لنا، فإذا انا بموسى عليه السلام، فرحب ودعا لى بخير.

ثم عرج إلى السماء السابعة، فاستفتح جبريل، فقيل: من هذا؟ قال: جبريل، قيل ومن معك؟ قال: محمد صلى الله عليه وسلم، قيل: وقد بعث إليه؟ قال: قد بعث إليه ففتح لنا، فإذا انا بإبراهيم عليه السلام مسندًا ظهره إلى البيت المعمور، وإذا هو يدخله كل يوم سبعون الف ملك، لا يعودون إليه.

ثم ذهب بى إلى السدرة المنتهى، وإذا ورقها كآذان الفيلة، وإذا ثمرها كالقلال، قال: فلما غشيها من امر الله ما غشى تغيرت، فما احد من خلق الله يستطيع ان ينعتها من حسنها، فاوحى الله إلى ما اوحى، ففرض على خمسين صلاةً فى كل يوم وليلة.

فنزلت إلى موسى عليه السلام، فقال: ما فرض ربك على امتك؟ قلت: خمسين صلاةً، قال: ارجع إلى ربك فاساله التخفيف، فإن امتك لا يطيقون ذلك، فإنى قد بلوت بنى إسرائيل وخبرتهم، قال: فرجعت إلى ربى، فقلت: يا رب، خفف على امتى، فحط عنى خمسًا، فرجعت إلى موسى، فقلت: حط عنى خمسًا، قال: إن امتك لا يطيقون ذلك، فارجع إلى ربك فاساله التخفيف، قال: فلم ازل ارجع بين ربى تبارك وتعالى، وبين موسى عليه السلام، حتى قال: يا محمد، إنهن خمس صلوات كل يوم وليلة، لكل صلاة عشر، فذلك خمسون صلاةً ومن هم بحسنة، فلم يعملها، كتبت له حسنةً،

فإن عملها، كتبت له عشرًا، ومن هم بسيئة فلم يعملها، لم تكتب شيئًا، فإن عملها، كتبت سيئةً واحدةً.

قال: فنزلت حتى انتهيت إلى موسى عليه السلام، فاخبرته، فقال: ارجع إلى ربك فاساله التخفيف، فقال رسول الله صلى الله عليه وسلم، فقلت: قد رجعت إلى ربى حتى استحييت منه.

Narrated by Anas bin Malik (RA): The Messenger of Allah (PBUH) said:

'Buraq was brought to me. It was a white animal, larger than a donkey but smaller than a mule. It would place its hooves where its sight reached. I mounted it and reached Bayt al-Maqdis. There, I tied it to the ring where the other Prophets used to tie their animals. Then I entered the Masjid and prayed two rak'ahs. After that, I came out, and Gabriel (AS) brought two vessels, one containing wine and the other containing milk. I chose the milk, and Gabriel (AS) said, 'You have chosen the fitrah (natural disposition).'

Then Gabriel (AS) ascended with me to the heavens. When we reached the first heaven, he asked the gatekeepers to open the gate. They asked, 'Who is it?' Gabriel replied, 'It is Gabriel.' They asked, 'Who is with you?' He replied, 'Muhammad (PBUH).' They asked, 'Has he been sent for?' Gabriel replied, 'Yes.' The gate was then opened for us.

When we entered, I saw Adam (PBUH). He welcomed me and prayed for my well-being.

Then Gabriel (AS) ascended with me to the second heaven. When we reached the second heaven, he asked the gatekeepers to open the gate. They asked, 'Who is it?' Gabriel replied, 'It is Gabriel.' They asked, 'Who is with you?' He replied, 'Muhammad (PBUH).' They asked, 'Has he been sent for?' Gabriel replied, 'Yes.' The gate was then opened for us. When the gate was opened, I saw Jesus (PBUH) and John (PBUH), who were maternal cousins. They welcomed me and prayed for my well-being.

Then Gabriel (AS) ascended with me to the third heaven. When we reached the third heaven, he asked the gatekeepers to open the gate. They asked, 'Who is it?' Gabriel replied, 'It is Gabriel.' They asked, 'Who is with you?' He replied, 'Muhammad (PBUH).' They asked, 'Has he been sent for?' Gabriel replied, 'Yes.' The gate was then opened for us. There, I saw Joseph (PBUH), who had been given half of all beauty. He welcomed me and prayed for my well-being.

Then Gabriel (AS) ascended with me to the fourth heaven. When we reached the fourth heaven, he asked the gatekeepers to open the gate. They asked, 'Who is it?' Gabriel replied, 'It is Gabriel.' They asked, 'Who is with you?' He replied, 'Muhammad (PBUH).' They asked, 'Has he been sent for?' Gabriel replied, 'Yes.' The gate was then opened for us and I saw Idris (PBUH). He welcomed me and prayed for my well-being. Allah says: 'And We raised him to a high station.'

Then Gabriel (AS) ascended with me to the fifth heaven. When we reached the fifth heaven, he asked the gatekeepers to open the gate. They asked, 'Who is it?' Gabriel replied, 'It is Gabriel.' They asked, 'Who is with you?' He replied, 'Muhammad (PBUH).' They asked, 'Has he been sent for?' Gabriel replied, 'Yes.' The gate was then opened for us. There, I saw Aaron (PBUH). He welcomed me and prayed for my well-being.

Then Gabriel (AS) ascended with me to the sixth heaven. When we reached the sixth heaven, he asked the gatekeepers to open the gate. They asked, 'Who is it?' Gabriel replied, 'It is Gabriel.' They asked, 'Who is with you?' He replied, 'Muhammad (PBUH).' They asked, 'Has he been sent for?' Gabriel replied, 'Yes.' The gate was then opened for us. There, I saw Moses (PBUH). He welcomed me and prayed for my well-being. When I moved forward, he began to cry. He was asked, 'What makes you weep?' Moses (PBUH) replied, 'O Lord, this young man was sent as a Prophet after me, and more of his followers will enter Paradise than mine.'

Then Gabriel (AS) ascended with me to the seventh heaven. When we reached the seventh heaven, he asked the gatekeepers to open the gate. They asked, 'Who is it?' Gabriel replied, 'It is Gabriel.' They asked, 'Who is with you?' He replied, 'Muhammad (PBUH).' They asked, 'Has he been sent for?' Gabriel replied, 'Yes.' The gate was then opened for us. There, I saw Abraham (PBUH), reclining against al-Bayt al-Ma'mur (the frequently visited house). Every day, seventy thousand angels enter it, and they never return to it again.

Then Gabriel (AS) took me to Sidrat al-Muntaha. Its leaves were like the ears of elephants, and its fruits were like large clay pots. When the tree was covered by the command of Allah, its beauty became indescribable. Then Allah revealed to me what He wished to reveal, and fifty prayers were enjoined upon me for every day and night.

As I descended and reached by Moses (PBUH), he asked, 'What has your Lord made obligatory upon your Ummah?' I replied, 'Fifty prayers have been made obligatory upon my Ummah.' He said, 'Go back to your Lord and ask for a reduction, for your Ummah will not be able to bear it. I have tested the Israelites and know this from experience.'

So I returned to my Lord and said, 'O my Lord, reduce the burden on my Ummah.' Allah reduced the number by five prayers. I returned to Moses (PBUH) and said, 'Allah has reduced it by five prayers for me.' He said, 'Your Ummah will still not be able to bear it. Go back to your Lord and ask for further reduction.' I kept going back and forth between my Lord and Moses (PBUH), until Allah said, 'O Muhammad! They are five prayers every day and night, but each prayer will be rewarded as ten, making them equivalent to fifty. My decree does not change.'

Allah further said, 'If someone intends to do a good deed but does not carry it out, a single good deed will be recorded for them. If they carry it out, ten good deeds will be recorded for them. If someone intends to do a bad deed but does not carry it out, nothing will be recorded against them. However, if they commit the bad deed, only one sin will be recorded.'

The Prophet (PBUH) said: "I then descended and returned to Moses (PBUH), who again said, 'Go back to your Lord and ask for further reduction.' I replied, 'I feel shy to keep going back to my Lord.'

Appendix 11 : Comparative Table of Five Principal Narratives

Hadith Source	Bukhari, No. 7517	Bukhari, No. 349	Bukhari, No. 3887	Muslim, No. 429	Nasa'i, No. 448
Book	Kitab al-Tawhid	Kitab al-Salah	Kitab Manaqib al-Ansar	Kitab al-Iman	Kitab al-Salah
Hadith Grade	Sahih	Sahih	Sahih	Sahih	Sahih
Companion Narrator	Anas bin Malik	Anas bin Malik, Abu Dharr al-Ghifari	Anas bin Malik, Malik bin Sa'sa'ah	Anas bin Malik	Anas bin Malik, Malik bin Sa'sa'ah
Tabi'i Narrator	Sharik bin Abdullah	Ibn Shihab	Qatadah	Thabit al-Bunani	Qatadah
Arrival of Three Angels Before *Mi'raj*	One night, three angels came, identified the Prophet, and then left.	Not mentioned	Not mentioned	Not mentioned	Not mentioned
Time of *Mi'raj*	Night	Not mentioned	Not mentioned	Not mentioned	Not mentioned
Location of the Prophet	Masjid al-Haram	The Prophet's house (Makkah)	Hatim in Masjid al-Haram	Not mentioned	Near the Kaaba
Opening of the Roof	The roof of the Prophet's house was opened	Not mentioned	Not mentioned	Not mentioned	Not mentioned
State of the Prophet	The Prophet was asleep, but his heart was awake.	Not mentioned	The Prophet was asleep.	Not mentioned	The Prophet was in a semi-sleep state.
Arrival of Angel	Not mentioned	Gabriel arrived	Gabriel arrived	Not mentioned	One angel arrived

Hadith Source	Bukhari, No. 7517	Bukhari, No. 349	Bukhari, No. 3887	Muslim, No. 429	Nasa'i, No. 448
Splitting of the Chest (*Shaq al-Sadr*)	The angels took the Prophet to the Zamzam well. Gabriel opened the chest and washed the interior with *Zamzam* water. The chest was filled with faith and wisdom and sealed.	Gabriel opened the chest, washed it with Zamzam, placed a tray filled with faith inside, then sealed it.	Gabriel opened the chest, removed the heart, placed it in a tray, washed it, and returned it.	Not mentioned	The chest was opened, the heart was washed with Zamzam, the heart was filled with faith and wisdom.
Riding Buraq	Not mentioned	Not mentioned	The Prophet rode Buraq	The Prophet rode Buraq	The Prophet rode Buraq
Observation of Bayt al-Maqdis	Not mentioned	Not mentioned	Not mentioned	The Prophet reached Bayt al-Maqdis. The Buraq was tied outside. The Prophet prayed two rak'ahs. Milk and wine were presented; he chose milk.	Not mentioned
Ascent to the Heavens	Gabriel took the Prophet to the first heaven.	Gabriel held the Prophet's hand and ascended.	The Prophet and Gabriel ascended together.	The Prophet and Gabriel ascended together.	The Prophet and Gabriel ascended together.

Hadith Source	Bukhari, No. 7517	Bukhari, No. 349	Bukhari, No. 3887	Muslim, No. 429	Nasa'i, No. 448
First Heaven	The Prophet met Adam.	The Prophet met Adam. He saw rivers like the Nile and Euphrates and Kawthar.	The Prophet met Adam.	The Prophet met Adam.	The Prophet met Adam.
Second Heaven	The Prophet met Idris.	The Prophet met Idris, Jesus, and Moses on different heavens.	The Prophet met Jesus and John.	The Prophet met Jesus and John.	The Prophet met Jesus and John.
Third Heaven	Not mentioned	Not mentioned	The Prophet met Joseph.	The Prophet met Joseph.	The Prophet met Joseph.
Fourth Heaven	The Prophet met Aaron.	Not mentioned	The Prophet met Idris.	The Prophet met Idris.	The Prophet met Idris.
Fifth Heaven	The Prophet saw another Prophet.	Not mentioned	The Prophet met Aaron.	The Prophet met Aaron.	The Prophet met Aaron.
Sixth Heaven	The Prophet saw Abraham.	The Prophet met Ibrahim.	The Prophet met Moses.	The Prophet met Moses.	The Prophet met Moses.
Seventh Heaven	The Prophet saw Moses.	Not mentioned	The Prophet met Abraham.	The Prophet met Abraham near Bayt al-Ma'mur.	The Prophet met Abraham and approached Bayt al-Ma'mur.
Observation of Sidrat al-Muntaha	The Prophet reached	Sidrat al-Muntaha was	The Prophet reached	The Prophet reached	Sidrat al-Muntaha was

Hadith Source	Bukhari, No. 7517	Bukhari, No. 349	Bukhari, No. 3887	Muslim, No. 429	Nasa'i, No. 448
	Sidrat al-Muntaha.	brought before the Prophet. The Prophet saw the Nile and Euphrates in river forms. Bayt al-Ma'mur was shown to the Prophet. Milk and wine were presented; he chose milk.	Sidrat al-Muntaha.	Sidrat al-Muntaha.	brought before the Prophet. The Prophet saw the Nile and Euphrates in river forms.
Hearing Angels' Pens	Not mentioned	The Prophet ascended further and heard the sound of the angels' pens.	Not mentioned	Not mentioned	Not mentioned
Divine Proximity	The Prophet came so close to Allah as two bows' length or closer.	Not mentioned	Not mentioned	Not mentioned	Not mentioned
Divine Revelation	Allah revealed to the Prophet.	Not mentioned	Not mentioned	Allah revealed to the Prophet.	Not mentioned
Obligation of 50 Prayers	Allah made 50 prayers obligatory.	50 prayers were made obligatory.	Allah made 50 prayers obligatory.	Allah made 50 prayers obligatory.	Allah made 50 prayers obligatory.
Moses Advising	Moses advised	Moses advised	Moses advised	Moses advised	Moses advised

Hadith Source	Bukhari, No. 7517	Bukhari, No. 349	Bukhari, No. 3887	Muslim, No. 429	Nasa'i, No. 448
Reduction of Prayers	reducing the number of prayers during the return.	reducing the number of prayers during the return.	reducing the number of prayers during the return.	reducing the number of prayers.	reducing the number of prayers.
Request to Allah for Reduction	The Prophet returned to Allah and requested a reduction in prayers.	The Prophet returned to Allah and requested a reduction in prayers.	The Prophet returned to Allah and requested a reduction in prayers.	The Prophet returned to Allah and requested a reduction in prayers.	The Prophet returned to Allah and requested a reduction in prayers.
Reduction in Prayers	10 prayers were reduced.	Some prayers were reduced.	10 prayers were reduced.	5 prayers were reduced.	10 prayers were reduced.
Moses Advising Further Reduction	Moses gave the same advice again.	Moses gave the same advice again.	Moses gave the same advice again.	Moses gave the same advice again.	Moses gave the same advice again.
Acceptance of Musa's Advice by the Prophet	The Prophet accepted the advice and returned to Allah.	The Prophet accepted the advice and returned to Allah.	The Prophet accepted the advice and returned to Allah.	The Prophet accepted the advice and returned to Allah.	The Prophet accepted the advice and returned to Allah.
Repeated Advice by Moses and Prophet's Return	The Prophet repeatedly returned upon Moses's advice.	The Prophet repeatedly returned upon Moses's advice.	The Prophet repeatedly returned upon Moses's advice.	The Prophet repeatedly returned upon Moses's advice.	The Prophet repeatedly returned upon Moses's advice.
Final Obligation of Five Prayers	Finally, Allah made five prayers obligatory with tenfold reward.	Finally, Allah made five prayers obligatory with tenfold reward.	Finally, Allah made five prayers obligatory.	Finally, Allah made five prayers obligatory with tenfold reward.	Finally, Allah made five prayers obligatory with tenfold reward for each.

Hadith Source	Bukhari, No. 7517	Bukhari, No. 349	Bukhari, No. 3887	Muslim, No. 429	Nasa'i, No. 448
Observation of Sidrat al-Muntaha After Obligations	Not mentioned	Then Gabriel took the Prophet to Sidrat al-Muntaha.	Not mentioned	Not mentioned	Not mentioned
Observation of Paradise	Not mentioned	Then the Prophet observed Paradise.	Not mentioned	Not mentioned	Not mentioned
Waking Up from Sleep	The Prophet woke up and found himself in Masjid al-Haram.	Not mentioned	Not mentioned	Not mentioned	Not mentioned

This Page Intentionally Left Blank

This Page Intentionally Left Blank

This Page Intentionally Left Blank